FROM THE
FRONT
LINES

Also by Joseph M. Stowell

Eternity
Radical Reliance
The Upside of Down

JOSEPH M. STOWELL

FROM THE FRONT LINES

PERSPECTIVES FROM
THE TRENCHES OF LIFE

Discovery House Publishers

Books, music, and videos that feed the soul with the Word of God

Box 3566 Grand Rapids, MI 49501

Discovery House Publishers is affiliated with RBC Ministries,
Grand Rapids, Michigan.

Discovery House books are distributed to the trade exclusively by
Barbour Publishing, Inc., Uhrichsville, Ohio.

Requests for permission to quote from this book should be directed to:
Permissions Department, Discovery House Publishers, P.O. Box 3566,
Grand Rapids, MI 49501.

Interior Design by Sherri L. Hoffman

CIP data available upon request

Printed in the United States of America

07 08 09 10 11/ CHG /10 9 8 7 6 5 4 3 2 1

CONTENTS

INTRODUCTION

In the classic comic strip *Pogo,* the character Pogo observes, "We have met the enemy, and he is us." I have to admit that I often had that in mind as I wrote the opening editorials in *Moody* magazine. I have a long-held belief that our struggles have more to do with ourselves and how we respond to life's challenges than the challenges themselves. So, feeling that it was unproductive to blast away at the enemies "out there," I determined to use the "Front Lines" column to help us get our own minds, hearts, and lives in order so that we could be effective for Jesus on the front lines of life.

As I wrote each piece, I was well aware that magazines don't last forever. While dog-eared copies and dated covers end up cluttering our coffee tables at home and the end tables at the doctor's office, they are ultimately destined for the dumper. So I was resigned to the fate that my feeble attempts at wisdom for life would soon be destined for the local incinerator. But thanks to the good people at Discovery House Publishers, the editorials have been rescued from that fate and put into this volume. And, I have to admit, since God's Word is true, and that truth is timeless, and life is really about the same issues over and over again, they continue to have the feeling of, "Hmmm . . . this might just be a help to someone after all!"

So here they are, the best of them, in book form. They come to you with the prayer that each article will meet you just where you are and that the Spirit will use them to equip you with increasing wisdom, hope, and courage as you face life on the front lines. The Holy Spirit's best way of equipping us for life in the trenches is supplying us with the whole armor of God. So, you will find that the articles have been divided into sections representing each of the different pieces of armor in Ephesians 6:13–17. The articles in part 1, "Having Fastened On the Belt of Truth," focus on how we align our own thoughts with God's thoughts as we come to an understanding of the truths of God's Word. Part 2, "Having Put On the Breastplate of Righteousness," addresses the matter of the human heart and God's ways of protecting our emotional well-being. The different ways that we share the good news of the gospel and live as salt and light is the subject of part 3, "As Shoes for Your Feet . . . the Gospel of Peace." "Take Up the Shield of Faith," part 4, reminds us that our actions are based on God—who He is and what He has promised to do rather than on outward circumstances. The articles in part 5, "Take Up the Helmet of Salvation," remind us to renew our minds as we enjoy freedom from old thoughts and habits. And finally, we see the authority and power of the Word of God in "Take the Sword of the Spirit."

It will soon become clear to you that some of these pieces were written in response to national, church, and personal situations that were current at the time. So, in a sense, they are a peek into history. But the truth and principles embedded in those moments of time remain as fresh and helpful for us today as they were then. It's my prayer that these quick reads will be greatly used of God to fortify and strengthen your life to live for His glory on the front lines!

—JOE STOWELL

PART ONE

HAVING FASTENED ON THE BELT OF TRUTH

IS GOD CUTE, OR WHAT?

In an August 25, 1997, *Time* magazine essay, Barbara Ehrenreich observed that "Our desire to make the awesome adorable is spoiling the mysteries of life." Among her examples is the way NASA named the rocks on Mars "Yogi," "Scooby Doo," and "Barnacle Bill" as though, she notes, "Someone high up in NASA must have issued a firm directive: 'Keep it cuddly, guys.'"

I was hoping she hadn't noticed how our modern brand of Christianity has trivialized the awesome God whom we should rightly adore. Much to my dismay, she had. "Watch one of our shlockier televangelists, and you'll be introduced to an affable deity eager to be enlisted as your personal genie. Yes, the Great Spinner of Galaxies, Digger of Black Holes is available, for a suitable 'love offering,' to relieve the itch of hemorrhoids and help you prevail in office intrigues!"

She concludes, "At least the ancient Hebrews had the good sense to make Yahweh unnamable and unseeable except in the flames of a burning bush."

Our evangelical culture tends to take the awesome reality of a transcendent God who is worthy to be feared and downsize Him so He could fit into our "buddy system." The way we talk about Him, the way we pray, and, more strikingly, the way we live shows that we have somehow lost our sense of being appropriately awestruck in the presence of a holy and all-powerful God. It's been a long time since we've heard a good sermon on the "fear of God."

If God were to show up visibly, many of us think we'd run up to Him and high-five Him for the good things He has done . . . or hug Him . . . or ask Him for an answer to that nagging theological question . . . or demand He tell us why that tragedy in our lives was permitted to rob us of our happiness and comfort. We would do none of these things. We would fall trembling at His feet as His awesome, mighty, and fearful glory filled the room.

Encounters with God have always had a sobering, shocking effect on people. Consider Adam and Eve in the garden after they sinned. Their response was to hide in shame. Moses had to remove his shoes before the burning bush because he was standing on holy ground. Later in Moses' life, he would have to be shielded in the cleft of the rock so he wouldn't see God's face. The prophet Isaiah fell down before God in agonizing awareness of the sins of his lips.

God in His mercy and grace calmed their fear and remediated their sinfulness. Nevertheless, their responses prove it is an awful thing, in a good sort of way, for men and women to come before the almighty and holy God of the universe.

In a good sort of way, because if we don't recognize how awesomely holy He is, we never see our sinfulness as it really is. Instead we live with a distorted, unhealthy view of ourselves that never humbly sees its need for mercy and grace.

Without a right sense of how big He is—in every way—we never know how frail and small we really are. If we live with an inaccurate sense of our size, we never know how much we need His presence, strength, wisdom, and support.

If we don't celebrate His transcendence and true significance, we deceive ourselves into believing that our own endeavors, aspirations, and accomplishments are the truly significant things in our world.

Simply put, any downsizing of God distorts our perspective on ourselves and on the life we live.

That is why Scripture is punctuated with calls to fear God, such as, "The fear of the Lord is the beginning of knowledge" (Proverbs 1:7). Ecclesiastes notes that after trying to find meaning in his wealth, work, and pleasure, the writer is left to conclude that the only thing of real value in life is to "fear God and keep His commandments" (Ecclesiastes 12:13).

It's time we called ourselves back to a sense of the majesty and wonder of a God who, though descending to meet us where we are, nevertheless is the God whose nature and stature are worthy of our respect, allegiance, and awe. Living in a state of awe refocuses our lives and stimulates grateful worship and praise to His worthy name.

IS IT THE GIFT OR THE GIVER?

Self-sufficiency may be as American as apple pie and mother-hood, but from God's point of view, it's a deep offense. When confronted with most "self" words, we melt with guilt. Charges of self-centeredness, self-enhancement, and a host of similar concepts often bring immediate conviction. But mention self-sufficiency, and we might actually feel proud of ourselves.

As I read Christ's letter in Revelation 3 to the church in Laodicia, I am struck that of all these seven letters, it held the strongest reproof. This is particularly intriguing since the other letters reprove churches for not loving Him, permitting false teachers to influence them, and looking the other way when some encouraged sexual immorality. I find myself wondering what could be more offensive to Christ than such violations.

Christ leaves little to the imagination when He says the Laodiceans' self-sufficient attitude is intolerably distasteful. You probably remember the passage. It's so graphic that once it is read, it is rarely forgotten. The Laodiceans are, Christ says, neither hot nor cold, but lukewarm in His mouth. They are like tea. It's great hot. It's terrific cold. But it is absolutely terrible at room temperature. As a result, Christ warns them He is ready to spit them out of His mouth. If you have ever had something in your mouth that gags you, your instinct is to expel it. The water supply in Laodicia was especially repulsive if served neither hot nor cold. The Laodiceans knew exactly what Christ was referring to.

But what was it in their lives that warranted such a response? Christ explains in Revelation 3:17, "You say, I am rich, I have prospered, and I need nothing." These believers found their sufficiency in all they had amassed. They thought they had all they needed. They didn't sense their need for Jesus Christ.

We all share the Laodiceans' capacity to live as though we don't need God. Oh, we know that we need Him. We've been taught that all of our lives. But do we live as if we *believe* we need Him? Let's be real. For most of us, God is little more than the 911 number of our lives. We easily lapse into thinking we really do have all we need. We have sufficient gifts and talents to succeed. Enough money to pay the bills and have a little fun. Friends. Health. Education. A career. And God, who will be there in case we need Him.

Let's remember that all we have—and all we feel sufficient about—are gifts of His grace towards us. Self-sufficiency ultimately comes down to loving the gift more than the Giver. In fact, the gift often eclipses the Giver as the source of our true satisfaction and security. What would we do if all God's gifts were stripped from our possession? What would we have then?

God rightly intends to be the focus of our hearts' dependency and desire. His gifts should inspire our gratitude and worship, not careless forgetfulness.

God deserves to be our ultimate point of dependence and desire. To regard Him as anything less is to send a message to Him about His ultimate worth and value in our lives. This is the sin of a self-sufficient view of life.

The greatest insult to loved ones is to ignore them or to make them feel unnecessary and unwanted until you need them. God feels the insult when we try to live self-sufficient lives. He must be more than one of many resources we call on to make life work for us. He deserves to be the preeminent focus of our dependence.

Christ confronts us with our true condition when He says, "[You do not realize] that you are wretched, pitiable, poor, blind and naked"(Revelation 3:17). Like the emperor who had no clothes, we have assumed that we are fully clothed in all that makes us feel sufficient. Yet Christ says that without a radical reliance on

Him, we are spiritually naked and in need of the gold, clothing, and eye salve that only He can give.

I grew up singing the hymn, "I need Thee, O I need Thee; Every hour I need Thee; O bless me now, my Savior, I come to Thee." It's time to humbly repent of the self-sufficiency in our lives and to revive that refrain in our hearts.

SUPPORT THE TROOPS!

As the war in Iraq drags into its fifth year, we are all worn out from the complex battle that continues to wage there. The tired troops want to come home, but with courage and dedication to the cause, they remain on the front lines. Those of us watching from a distance do what we can to support them, driving around with our "Support the Troops" stickers on our cars and praying fervently for their safety and success.

No one can accurately predict the resolution, but the war carries a poignant lesson for all those who care about the cause of Jesus Christ. As God's people, we are engaged in a war of far greater proportions—warfare against the hierarchies and unseen powers of the satanic hosts (Ephesians 6:10–12). This battle concerns the liberation of the eternally lost, the advancement of Christ's kingdom, and the glory of His name.

What strikes me is the surprising lack of support for the front-line men and women who are in the trenches waging this war against the gates of hell. Some of our spiritual troops are dug in on battlefields far away. From massive urban centers like Hong Kong and Rio de Janeiro to the remote jungles of Papua, New Guinea, among executives and shopkeepers and natives, these soldiers are penetrating enemy territory with the life-changing claims of Christ.

I am frequently brought face-to-face with the everyday struggles of missionaries who serve as soldiers in the work of the kingdom. Some spend an inordinate amount of time getting to the front lines because the funds they need are not available. Others often feel forgotten and neglected during their stint on the field. When they finally come home, they feel that somehow they don't fit.

I also have the privilege to talk heart-to-heart with pastors who labor in their homelands. While some feel loved and supported, others speak of the difficulty they face in trying to focus their church's attention on the advancement of the gospel. Often a pastor is the target of bickering and petty agendas that turn the congregation inward and end up dividing and sapping its strength.

Laymen fight it out in the trenches of the marketplace, both in day-to-day work where they seek to minister for Jesus and in more formal settings of Bible studies and luncheons for businesspeople. Yet many find little enthusiasm or support for what they are doing in the touch arena of secular society.

So, as Americans commemorate Memorial Day, I think it's fitting to stop and consider how we are doing in terms of spiritual warfare. Let's take Paul's advice to "put on the whole armor of God, that you may be able to stand against the schemes of the devil" (Ephesians 6:11). If each of us were to make a personal commitment to put away what is petty and temporary and instead concentrate on what will advance the cause of Christ, think of the ground we could claim for His kingdom! If we pledge to pray consistently and specifically for those involved on the front lines, we will provide a vital aspect of support. And if we put our money where we say our hearts are, we will keep the battle lines supplied.

The big difference, of course, between earth-side battles and spiritual battles, is that we already know the outcome. Jesus already claimed eternal victory, and in the meantime He gives us the power for victory in the skirmishes we face along the way. So enlist yourself today, and don't forget to support the troops!

DEALING WITH THE "D WORD"

When you think of *doctrine*, what comes to mind?

For many of us, words like *dry, boring, deep, academic, irrelevant,* and *divisive* describe how we feel when the "D word" comes up in conversation. If we are given a choice in small group discussion topics of finances, family, marketplace, Christians in politics, culture wars, and doctrine, doctrine regularly ranks a solid last.

Perhaps it doesn't matter. Given how divisive doctrine can be and how pressing the other issues are, maybe we are better off not making a big deal out of it. Not really.

Doctrine, properly understood and applied, makes all the difference in the world of belief and behavior. Ultimately, we will be held accountable for our stewardship of truth revealed. To say nothing of the fact that the spiritual stability of the next generation depends largely on how well we have held and taught the fundamental tenets of orthodoxy.

How, then, have we developed our disdain for doctrine? The fault doesn't lie with doctrine. We have done to doctrine what backyard chefs often do to a good steak—ruin it in the making. If doctrine seems irrelevant, dry, and boring, it's only because we have taught it as a cognitive system of facts about God and have separated it from the most vital issues of life.

Our relationships at home grow out of a proper understanding of the doctrine of Christ (Ephesians 5). Moral purity is an extension of a right view of redemption (1 Corinthians 6). Worship is pawned from what we know about the attributes and attitudes of God. Servanthood and service are shallow and short-lived without an appreciation of the Incarnation (Philippians 2). Unity is tied to the Trinity (John 17). Security, to the person and work of the Holy

Spirit (Ephesians 4). Evangelism and the doctrines of the church are inseparable. Careers are rightly understood only in the context of eschatology (Matthew 6).

Our inability to see the transforming power of doctrine has left us with the impression that the details of truth are irrelevant and that we can discuss life-related issues productively apart from solid, unchanging foundations of truth. We have forgotten Christ's warning in the parable of the house built on the sand (Matthew 7:24–27).

We have also damaged ourselves by confusing our extended perspectives on doctrinal issues with the few core precepts that believers have embraced through the centuries. We have not done well in differentiating the truths we should go to the stake for and the beliefs we hold more loosely.

Our failure here is best seen when we trumpet the minutia of our doctrinal systems more loudly than the fundamentals on which they are based. This causes confusion among the saints and unnecessary division and belligerence among brothers. This may be the reason why some stand at a distance from doctrine.

The belligerence factor cannot be taken lightly. While it's important to protect doctrine and hold each other accountable, this must be done with love and concern. Too often the prophets in our land have spoken in such a way that their harshness and lack of fairness have precluded a hearing.

It doesn't help either that we live in a culture that holds tolerance in high esteem. Doctrinal truth is by nature intolerant of error. Truth defines and divides. Resisting these boundaries leads to the erosion of the very foundations upon which the church is built.

Orthodox truth is the most important commodity we have. If we ignore it, it just may go away. If we make it less of a priority, we weaken the fabric of the church. Without clear doctrine, there is no true evangelism. Without doctrine, our unity is built on slippery slopes.

Now more than ever, we must rise to embrace doctrine as our friend, allow it to transform our lives, defend it with grace and honor, and pass it on to our children that we might fulfill the call of the church to be the pillar and support for the truth (1 Timothy 3:15).

FROM VIRTUES TO VALUES
AND BACK AGAIN

Character has become a lost commodity. In fact, it is so lost that we find it hard to define what it means. In earlier days, character was what you had when you unflinchingly lived by the commonly held virtues of society. But character vanishes when there are no virtues. America, and in some respects the church, has lost its sense of virtue.

I hadn't even heard the word *virtues* for a long time until William Bennett published his book by that title. I remember purchasing a copy when it first came out and saying to the young, trendy, intellectual-looking clerk, "This will probably be a best-seller." To which he replied, "I hope not."

His reply was enigmatic to me until I read a fascinating book by Gertrude Himmelfarb entitled *The Demoralization of Society.* She traces the intentional, philosophical shift away from the concept of *virtue* to the now commonly accepted term, *value.* Virtue relates to behavior that is morally best, that which conforms to a common moral authority. A value, on the other hand, relates to a personal set of preferences that I as an individual have determined as the standard by which I will measure my choices and my accountability.

Through the past several decades, we have seen the steady erosion of a common moral authority in America. In the past, this agreement to the basic moral codes of Moses and Christ was the standard by which we all were measured. Cultural absolutes gave us targets to aim at. The social order honored integrity, hard work, loyalty, faithfulness to family, respect for authority, sexual purity, selfless compassion, and other morally constructive commodities. These were absolutes. They were our virtues.

Recently, however, virtues such as these have been marked for extinction by those who speak powerfully through music, movies, TV dramas, sitcoms, and media commentaries. Relativists have also flooded our educational system, telling our children that because there are no moral absolutes, they can choose their own set of values by which to live.

Few people seem to link the rise in violence, crime, disease, disorientation, the breakdown of the family, and the increase in despair to this shift from virtues to values. But it's hard to ignore the fact that we have lost much as a country since we became so "enlightened," since we lost our virtue.

Even more troublesome, this shift from virtues to values is evident in the mindset of many Christians. We talk about the importance of values. We verbalize our concern for family values and the return of morality to America. But I often get the impression that we count these to be *our* values, choices that *we* have made from a range of available options.

George Barna notes that in a recent survey of Americans, 71 percent said they don't believe in absolutes. What is shocking is that 40 percent of evangelical Christians don't either.

I sometimes hear Christians say things like, "Well, I believe it's wrong for me, but I can't say it's wrong for everyone else." Whenever we say that, we are talking values, not virtues. That kind of thinking neutralizes the compelling power of righteousness. It disables us from calling our children and our culture to a clear understanding of God's standard of behavior, by which we all will be measured.

Our moral authority is nothing less than God Himself. He is true, just, loving, merciful, pure, faithful, and benevolent. His nature establishes the absolute standard.

The qualities that comprise His character are not simply things that comprise *our* values. They are the essence of what is correct for all of society, for all mankind. They are the measures of character, respectability, stability, and safety.

If we His people lose our sense of absolute virtue, we will lose not only our character, but also our opportunity to bring a healing voice to a hurting world. We will compromise the very nature of His correct and changeless glory reflected through our lives.

May we instead be people who unashamedly cling to the absolutes of God's character and who by our own lives call others to virtue again.

The psalmist celebrated virtue when he said, "Oh how I love your law! It is my meditation all the day . . . I hold back my feet from every evil way, in order to keep your word" (Psalm 119:97, 101).

THE TRUTH ABOUT UNITY

The psalmist had it right when he exclaimed, "How good and pleasant it is when brothers dwell in unity!" (133:1). He obviously knew what many of us already know, that harmony in relationships is one of life's greatest rewards. But unity is important not simply because it is fulfilling and satisfying to us, it also rates high on God's agenda.

So let me go on record as an avid proponent of Christian unity. It gives me serious pause when I read in Scripture that there are six things that the Lord hates, in fact seven that are an abomination to Him. The final item on this list of behaviors abominable to the Lord is when someone "sows discord among brothers" (Proverbs 6:19).

Or consider the Lord's prayer on behalf of His disciples and all those who would follow them (John 17:11–21). Jesus prayed that His followers would show the world that He and the Father were one by being one among themselves.

If Christians are to be true to our God and an accurate reflection of Him to our world, then oneness must be a major item on our agenda. Those who cause division in the church over matters of power and control need to be confronted with the fact their desire to rule at the expense of unity is a sin against the body of Christ.

Believers who use legitimate differences of preference or denominational distinctives to draw lines of separation in the body sin against the very body they seek to protect. It is ironic that some of us, in our zeal to keep the church pure, end up polluting Christ's body with unwarranted divisions.

But unity should not be pursued at any cost. There is something more important than unity, and that is truth. We dare not sacrifice truth on the altar of unity. Christ made this clear in His prayer for His disciples. Before He prayed for their unity, He prayed they be set apart in the truth He had taught them. Once they were firmly established in the truth, they could forge their unity in the truth they all affirmed.

If Christians lose the importance of truth in the pursuit of unity, then we will eventually lose truth. Yet, at the end of the day, all we have is truth. It is the truth that defines and guides all that we do and all that we are. Doctrines that biblically define salvation, Christ's deity and bodily resurrection, His virgin birth, and the infallible authority of Scripture are all non-negotiables; they are central to our faith.

Attempting to unite spiritually with those who are not of the truth or promoting spiritual endeavors with them says, in essence, that truth is no longer important. I remember talking with a well-meaning Christian woman who asked me, "Have you ever prayed with a Mormon?" It was quite clear that she had—and that she believed that what she felt as they prayed together had made them legitimately one. The problem is that Mormons deny the deity of Christ. The apostle John makes it dramatically clear in his second epistle that anyone who denies Christ cannot be of Christ and, as such, should not be received as one with us in Christ.

To protect the truth of the gospel from those who would corrupt it by adding good works as a means to eternal life, the apostle Paul declares in no uncertain terms that those who bring another gospel are "accursed" (Galatians 1:8).

If we accept a muddled version of the gospel for the sake of achieving "unity" with those who misrepresent it, we will eventually lose the gospel. That is a price we can't afford to pay.

Together we celebrate the importance of redemptive truth in a truthless world that so desperately needs a clear voice about the finished work of Christ.

SURRENDERING TO THE INTERRUPTIONS

Did you ever wonder how much you might get done if it weren't for the interruptions? My day usually begins before anyone else is stirring in our home. When I emerge from sleep, the first thing on my agenda is to make my way to the coffee-maker, whose advanced-timer technology has the coffee warmed and waiting for me.

I fill my favorite mug, find my way to the living room, and park in my favorite chair. After a brief time of prayer and meditation, I think through the day that stretches out before me and create a plan to accomplish the critical tasks.

In my younger, more idealistic years, I honestly believed at the beginning of the day that I could accomplish all that I planned to do. But reality has taught me that I rarely get everything finished. Not because of insufficient willpower or want-to, but because of the interruptions. That phone call at just the wrong time, the emergency that took me from my desk in the middle of my most productive moment, a knock at the door, or a distracting thought that derailed my heart and mind.

Even happy interruptions ultimately create havoc. Bane or blessing, interruptions always have a way of shredding a person's day.

If we are not careful, our response to most interruptions is a growing sense of irritation. But a glance toward God reminds us that He in His sovereignty may have different plans for our day. In fact He is a God who often interrupts us—and sometimes dramatically so.

Are we so far from Christmas that we have forgotten how God interrupted the plans of one couple in Nazareth? He chose them to be the parents to nurture His redemptive gift to mankind.

And let's not forget Paul's interruption on the Damascus road. Think of Moses' burning bush. Or consider Job, who endured a traumatic interruption to prove the worthiness of God before all of the spirit world and angelic host.

All of these people willingly surrendered to the divine interruption rather than resist it. They knew that if God interrupted their lives, it was for something bigger, better, and beyond their own plans.

Two weeks before Thanksgiving, Scott and Janet Willis, with six of their nine children, were returning home to Chicago after a daytrip to Wisconsin. As they drove through Milwaukee, their brand-new van hit a large piece of metal lying in the road. It punctured their gas tank, and immediately an explosion of flames engulfed them.

Scott and Janet called out to their children and tumbled from the van. Seriously burned themselves, they turned back to look. Five of their children had been consumed in the flames. The sixth would die later in the hospital.

"No!" Janet screamed as she helplessly watched the flames. Then her husband touched her shoulder and said, "Janet, this is what we've been prepared for."

"It was quick," he continued, "and they are with the Lord."

Later Janet explained that she knew he was right. His reminder quieted her heart.

Needless to say, this tragic interruption in the Willises' lives caught the attention of the media in the Midwest. So riveting was the story and so dramatic their faith, that the *Chicago Tribune* wrote of the family in one of its lead editorials.

It quoted Mr. Willis as saying, "I know God has purposes and God has reasons . . . God has demonstrated His love to us and our family. There is no question in our mind that God is good, and we praise Him in all things."

Quite frankly, I feel shallow and small for being irritated with the incidental and insignificant interruptions in my life. They are not worthy to be compared to the interruption that the Lord brought to Scott and Janet Willis.

But thanks to them and their faith, I am learning afresh an important lesson: that each day belongs to God and not to me. His sovereign wisdom and love render His plans far more significant than mine.

In those quiet, early moments in my living room when I have finished planning my day, it's important to yield it to Him, to see every interruption as a divinely scheduled event for His glory and gain.

Think of how much our God might get done if we surrendered to His interruptions.

THE TEST OF RELEVANCE

"Joe, if I hear the word *relevance* one more time, I think I will scream."

My friend's words echoed a feeling shared by many. At times it appears as if relevance has become the high calling and commission of the church.

I don't count myself among those who want to stop talking about relevance. But I am concerned that we define it biblically. Let me explain.

Relevance talk has surfaced because our culture has gone through dramatic changes in the past few decades. Given the change in morality, mindset, politics, and philosophy, the church finds itself scrambling to stay up to date. Like puppies chasing a darting squirrel, the church moves helter-skelter across the landscape of society, trying to keep up with changing times and thought.

In this society, absolutes are no longer in vogue, and tolerance of everything and anything is of high value. So it seems dreadfully irrelevant for Christians to maintain that some things are always right, that other things are always wrong, and that God will hold us accountable for violating the absolutes of His Word.

Our quest for relevance often leads us to say things like, "Well, I don't think it's right for me, but I can't say it's wrong for someone else." Such a statement, as innocent as it may seem, makes our beliefs and convictions nothing more than pragmatic choices of how we want to live. It discounts the reality of the unchanging principles of God's Word that apply to all mankind. It also undermines our capacity to serve as a source of conviction and an instrument of righteousness in our day.

Because our culture has decided to blur any distinctions between the genders, it seems irrelevant for Christians to maintain that God has assigned different roles for men and women, both in the church and in the home. Perhaps those distinctions wouldn't be too important, except that Scripture roots them in the vital truth about Christ's role in the church and His relationship with us (Ephesians 5:21–33).

Today's preaching, to maintain some vestige of relevance, rarely anchors its proclamation in "Thus saith the Lord." Instead, we are more prone to qualify biblical pronouncements with, "I think," "Wouldn't it be best," "Don't you think," or "Here's something you should give some thought to."

It seems irrelevant these days to be too conservative about morals. Christians gladly entertain themselves at the altar of mass media events—whether film, television, or music—that are not only undergirded by secular and often sinful principles but that openly proclaim them. We seem to be more worldly wise, less legalistic, and far more relevant if we free ourselves to traffic in the mainstream of media events. It does seem rather irrelevant, does it not, to "turn away from evil and do good" (1 Peter 3:11).

Our real problem is not relevance, but understanding what is truly relevant. In a recent forum, Calvin Miller, pastor, author, and Christian thinker, made this profound observation: The truth is what is really relevant. For truth, he declared, speaks about what is always and ultimately real. It is the only hope for meeting our real needs.

Throughout history, the church has done its best work when it has stood faithfully for what is true, when it has proclaimed it clearly and compassionately, and when it has lived it into the culture—even if that culture falsely defines truth or denies its existence.

Truth stands the test of time. And only truth has the power to transform a life. God Himself is true. Our only hope for having our deepest, most relevant needs met is to stop chasing the deceptive ways of the adversary and to anchor our lives unflinchingly in the center of God's unfailing truth.

The truly relevant Christian affirms truth at home, in the marketplace, in relationships, in proclamation, and in character.

This is the only way that the church can remain ultimately and finally relevant. While the world may say that we are irrelevant in our adherence to truth, in time all will know that the only relevant reality of both history and eternity is Jesus Christ and what He has taught.

For as Scripture affirms, the day is coming—even for those who have denied truth in their quest for relevance—when every knee shall bow and every tongue will confess that Jesus Christ is Lord.

IN SPIRIT AND IN TRUTH

In recent decades, we Christians have learned a lot about worship. The transition from a staid, cognitive expression of our faith has brought the church a fresh breath of spontaneity, enthusiasm, and joy. Today we freely lift our faces toward God with a radiance that reflects His love. Periodically, tears of repentance, release, and gratitude may flow down our cheeks.

No longer do we see the first half hour of our Sunday services merely as preliminaries or the sermon merely as teaching. Knowing that true worship means ascribing worth to God, we are learning to focus our hearts through songs and prayers on His character and His work as well as expressing His worth by submitting our minds and hearts to His Word as it is proclaimed.

While this movement toward true worship delights me, I must admit some concerns.

True worship draws us toward an intimate encounter with God and opens our hearts to a deeper, fuller understanding of who He is. When we draw near to God, we are inevitably struck with the holiness of His person. Like the prophet Isaiah, who saw a vision of the Lord "sitting upon a throne, high and lifted up" (Isaiah 6:1), we realize that we are unclean in His presence. Such worship compels us to repentance, purity, and grateful service.

Yet, now that we have restored worship to its proper place, the purity of the church is at an all-time low. And pastors say that one of their most difficult tasks is motivating the flock to serve in the kingdom.

This leads me to wonder if our worship has become little more than an enjoyable emotional outlet for us, something that fulfills our needs without focusing our attention on the incomparable

Christ. And while it's better to find emotional release in the church than in some of the options that the world offers, this is not the essence of worship.

I'm also concerned about our propensity for enthusiasm without edification. Recently, a friend told me he was attending a new church. The services were especially meaningful and fulfilling, he said, because they consisted almost entirely of worship.

"Doesn't the pastor preach?" I asked him.

"There's a ten-minute message," my friend explained. "It's helpful, but the real focus of the service is worship."

At best, enthusiasm without edification leaves us hollow. A church with warmth but little wonder. At worst, it leaves us vulnerable to seductive influences, both doctrinally and personally. Biblical worship is based on what we know to be true about God, yet many in the church today know very little of what Scripture teaches about God.

"Enter his gates with thanksgiving, and his courts with praise!" (Psalm 100:4) is preceded by, "Know that the Lord, he is God! It is he who made us, and we are his; we are his people, and the sheep of his pasture" (v. 3). Those are profound scriptural truths, providing a solid foundation for our worship.

Worship is a response, not a religious catharsis—a response to our experience with the Word and works of God that describe and illuminate the magnificent realities of God.

One of the most fervent worship experiences in Scripture took place on the banks of the Red Sea just after God had demonstrated His delivering power (Exodus 15:1–21). Concentrating on the truth of God's beneficial acts should stimulate our worship.

Now that we're finally moving in the right direction for worship, getting sidetracked would be unfortunate. We must not let our adversary distort this new priority on worship.

Perhaps we need to rekindle some of the great hymns that are so full of truth about God, which blend edification and enthusiasm into one experience. While I love worship choruses and find that they pull from my heart much of what I feel, I also treasure the substance and depth of our hymns.

In addition, it might be good to worship after the sermon. This option puts edification before enthusiasm. We could build the worship time around what we have learned about God, with vibrant testimonies of His work in our lives and fitting expressions of praise and thanksgiving.

Whatever methods of worship we choose, the passion of true praise must lead us to greater purity, participation, and a genuine enthusiasm growing out of edification.

We will know we have worshiped when it moves us toward a more profound awareness of our God.

GETTING IT STRAIGHT

Growing up in Hackensack, New Jersey, just across the George Washington Bridge from New York City, provided a variety of experiences for me. One was going to school with some of the rough kids from the neighboring town of South Hackensack.

I recall one afternoon, playfully sparring with one of the southside guys and having his punch actually land on my face. The blow jarred one of my front teeth loose. Thankfully, the dentist was able to anchor the tooth again, and I didn't lose it. In fact, I was better off—the tooth had always been crooked, so the dentist straightened it as he worked.

Sometimes the blows of life have a way of taking something crooked and making it straight. This just may be happening to the church in America today. While we are sitting around, licking our wounds from a series of political defeats, perhaps God wants to catch our attention and straighten some of our thinking.

Have we really thought that God intended government to be the purveyor of righteousness and the champion of truth? That's what we could expect of God's government in a theocracy, but not from fallen creatures in human government.

We are right to expect governmental leaders to be fair, honest, just, and moral. But we need to recognize that government most often operates on the planes of pragmatism, politics, self-advancement, and loose thinking about solid biblical values. We Americans have been spoiled to have a governmental system that was built on Judeo-Christian principles. That is a rare phenomenon in history.

Romans 13 assigns to government the roles of guaranteeing justice, peace, and safety. While that will never be carried out perfectly as long as imperfect people run government, it is what God expects. According to the same text, God expects us to submit to government authorities because He has appointed them. He commands us to pay taxes and give honor to those over us.

What puts this in bold relief is that the Roman Christians were living in an environment far more pagan than ours. Their government had no interest in righteousness or in the values of truth.

As 1 Timothy 2 indicates, God has established government to maintain a peaceful environment that is open to the free flow of the gospel. Why, then, are we so mad at our government? Why is there so little prayer and so little honor and so little submissiveness in our attitudes?

We don't have it straight. We have expected government to do what the church is called to do. Maybe one reason we are so upset is that we have been able to coast so long in our stewardship of righteousness and biblical values. Now that government has abandoned us, we will have to assume more of the responsibility ourselves.

Jesus was speaking to us, not to government, when He said, "Let your light shine before others, so that they may see your good works and give glory to your Father who is in heaven" (Matthew 5:16). We are the ones who are called to bring the power of God to a pagan world. Bill Clinton is not our national pastor. Congress is not denominational headquarters. We must understand what God has asked our governmental leaders to do, pray that they will do it well, honor them, and then get busy about the task that has been relegated to us.

It starts within our hearts, by cultivating a relationship with God that produces a Christlike spirit. That affects our home—our relationships to our spouse, our parents, and our children. As our homes begin to reflect the stability and joy that only righteousness can bring, our churches are also transformed. The change then spreads from our churches into our communities, as we become living advertisements for all that God is and all that He wants this world to be.

No matter how dark and brutish American society may become, it can never extinguish the light of Christlike hearts and homes and churches.

It's tragic that so many of us are known for our anger at government. We are quick to trash the leaders whom God has appointed over us. Part of being light in the darkness, part of our distinction in this world, is that we, unlike those with political agendas, will honor, submit, and pay taxes to our government with a good spirit.

This doesn't mean that we cease working to elect leaders who will govern in a godly and effective way. What it does mean is that we get it straight about who does what. The church must be the church and not expect the government to do what God has called us to do.

PLEASURE SEEKERS

Summer is a pleasure-seeker's delight. It's the season of beaches, boats, barbecues, and a hundred other possibilities. The Labor Day weekend offers the last chance to enjoy some of those summertime thrills.

Most of us, however, would have to admit that summer is not the only time we seek pleasure. An internal drive for pleasure pervades nearly every aspect of our lives. And our environment seduces us with "thrill-a-minute" options, promising that these hedonistic hot spots will provide ultimate fulfillment.

But as Solomon discovered, the search for pleasure is at best empty and meaningless. "Whatever my eyes desired I did not keep from them," he wrote. "I kept my heart from no pleasure . . . All was vanity and a striving after wind" (Ecclesiastes 2:10–11).

The ultimate results of hedonistic pursuits are often worse than meaningless. We feel shame, loss, guilt, and regret. Pleasure is not simply a pristine commodity on the playground of life. It is why people abuse, manipulate, rape, cheat, begin affairs, destroy children, and advance themselves at others' expense.

Scripture has a lot to say about the destructive influence of mismanaged pleasure. Proverbs 21:17 states, "Whoever loves pleasure will be a poor man." Hebrews describes pleasure as the short-term reward of sin (11:24–26). It can distract us from responding to God's Word (Luke 8:14). It destroys relationships (James 4:1) and distorts our prayer life (James 4:3).

Eventually, addiction to pleasure can eclipse our commitment to God. When listing the destructive life qualities of the end times, Paul included people who are "lovers of pleasure rather than lovers of God" (2 Timothy 3:4).

It's not that pleasure is out of bounds for God's people. First Timothy 6:17 states that God "richly provides us with everything to enjoy." Other passages speak of legitimate pleasure from food, laughter, friends, work, and the intimacy of a marriage relationship.

Pleasure itself is not the problem, but how we manage it.

God never intended pleasure to be a goal of our lives, but rather a by-product of significant and constructive pursuits. It comes from fulfilling what we were built to do. It's the joy of bringing happiness to others and knowing that God is pleased with us.

One of the predominant drives of children is to please their parents. Counselors tell us that children who grow up without feeling the joy of parental affirmation often become driven to perform, seeking to please someone, somewhere, somehow with some part of their lives. As a result, they may become twisted by unhealthy addictions to work or by immoral relationships. They may become weak and unprincipled, willing to violate biblical standards if it means they can finally win approval from someone.

This intrinsic drive to please the significant people in our lives reflects the fact that we were built to bring pleasure to someone outside of ourselves—God. The highest satisfaction of life is knowing in our spirits that He indeed is pleased with us. "We make it our aim to please him," Paul wrote (2 Corinthians 5:9).

Unlike some people we know, God is capable of being pleased. "The Lord takes pleasure in his people" (Psalm 149:4). He is pleased when we offer our bodies to Him as living sacrifices (Romans 12:1), as well as by our praise and our good deeds (Hebrews 13:15–16). Through living a life of non-negotiated obedience, produced by a faith that stands firm even in the face of the unknown, we can indeed know the joy of pleasing God.

Not surprisingly, Psalm 1 says that those who delight in doing the law of the Lord are truly happy and blessed. When we keep Christ's commands and abide in His love, our joy is complete (John 15:10–11).

This joy is not the short-lived, down-sided thrill package that our world offers. It is the long-term sense of stability and "all-rightness" that comes from a life bent on pleasing our heavenly Father.

It also involves a commitment to serving those around us. "Let each of us please his neighbor for his good, to build him up," Paul wrote (Romans 15:2). Christ "did not please himself," but gave His life so we'd have the pleasure of redemption (v. 3).

According to Luke, as the boy Jesus grew in wisdom and stature, He found favor with God *and* men (Luke 2:52). Our culture, so bent on pleasure at any cost, knows little of the true joy that comes from such a life.

Pleasure is not the goal of life, but the wonderful reward to those who live to love God and neighbor. Only then will we fully know the thrill of it all.

M y pastor tells the story of two men standing at the gates of heaven, debating whether God was black or white. Saint Peter, overhearing the discussion, told them to be patient, that they'd soon find out. When the gates opened, God said, "Buenos dias, señors."

While it's obvious that God transcends our color distinctives, the point of the story is important. We tend to assume that our world is *the* world, giving little thought to those who are different.

We live in a colorful world. And we who know Christ as Savior and Lord are on our way to a colorful heaven. Some from every tribe and nation will be there (Revelation 5:9). As citizens of heaven (Philippians 3:20), we are to live according to its standards and reflect its attitudes. That includes living now with brothers and sisters of all kinds.

Scripture also commands us to be followers of Christ. In a profound, multicultural moment in the New Testament, Jesus led His disciples through Samaria (John 4:1–42), a region they viewed as racially and religiously off limits. While the disciples went into town for food, Jesus remained at a public well. A woman came by, and He began to minister to her spiritual need.

The returning disciples were shocked. Not only was Christ willing to be in Samaria, but also He was willing to talk to a woman (no rabbi would have done that), and a Samaritan to boot.

But Christ held all humanity to be worthy of His saving grace. He cut across class lines, reaching out to the rich, to the beggar, to prostitutes. Once they came to Christ, they lived and moved in the community of believers with no further thought of the cultural distinctions that had divided them before.

When I was a boy, we sang a little song in Sunday school that went, "Red and yellow, black and white, all are precious in His sight." I don't know why we stop singing that song when we become adults. Perhaps it's too challenging. Could it be that we have been schooled by the divisive attitudes of our culture? Have our souls been enculturated instead of Christianized?

What a tremendous testimony Christians could provide if we were willing to shed our pride and prejudice and embrace one another with the color-blind and class-blind eyes and heart of our Lord and Savior.

This would require a good dose of repentance, not because we have all been intentionally divisive, but because many of us have simply been unintentional about cultivating a welcome for all in the body of Christ.

Some of us would have to repent of the bitterness we've held against those of different backgrounds who have subjugated us either in activity or attitude. In a fresh wave of forgiveness, we would need to seek restoration and reconciliation.

We should also have to recognize the systems and institutional structures that enhance division, that hinder people of the other side from becoming full partners with us in our churches, organizations, and endeavors.

This does not mean we should ignore our diversity. God has made us different on purpose with a purpose. We should celebrate who we are and what God has made us to be. And all of us should celebrate that for one another. Given the beauty and the strength of our diversity, we have the opportunity to bond that diversity together for the advance of Christ's kingdom and His glory. In our distinct ways and distinct cultures, we walk together behind Him and for Him.

It's time to be honest with ourselves and to be just with one another. It's time to be vulnerable and humble. It's time to raise the flag of harmony within the body of Christ.

Seldom has the world been so polarized in terms of race, class, and gender. What a privilege for us to demonstrate the reality of Christ by showing the world what His love can do. As society finds itself unable to bridge the gap of diversity, may the Lord hasten the day when we hear people asking us how we live and work so well together. It will then be our joy to say, "We thought you'd never ask. Let us tell you about Jesus Christ."

In that way we would fulfill the commission of Christ, who said, "Let your light shine before others, so that they may see your good works and give glory to your Father who is in heaven" (Matthew 5:16).

FEELING WORSE ABOUT OURSELVES

Though the politicians continue to tell us that we need change, one thing is sure: America has already changed.

The change is dramatic, and by most measures it is not for the better. Even a casual perusal of the daily newspaper reveals that the American dream is fading into a shadowy nightmare. More and more people are haunted by a loss of safety and hope in a world where stability and certainty are vanishing.

And those of us who are numbered among the redeemed feel increasingly disenfranchised, left out in the cold.

AIDS proliferates under the protection of political agendas, while those who speak to the causes and recommend cures such as abstention, monogamy, and heterosexuality are branded as naïve at best or as bigoted and homophobic at worst.

Abortion is now a politically protected choice. Those who challenge the issue from a perspective of morality are ignored or scoffed, and those who protest are marginalized or jailed. We murder our babies as a means of birth control, and society applauds it as progress.

Atheism, self-expression, and the endorsement and advancement of a variety of alternate lifestyles and societal philosophies form the agendas of the educational elite. The only forbidden entity is theism, with its conviction that there is a God and that His revealed values should at least be a player in the field of discussion.

In a supposedly sophisticated, intellectual environment that welcomes *all* ideas, it's interesting that ideas about God and His proven moral guidelines are not only ignored, but also banned.

It's not only we Christians who are feeling that the changes have disenfranchised us. Americans generally are restless and dissatisfied. It seems the more we change, the worse we feel about ourselves.

Forbes magazine recently celebrated its seventy-fifth anniversary with a volume of essays entitled *Why We Feel So Bad When We Have It So Good.* And by and large, Americans do have it "good." We live in the most affluent society in the world, yet even "a chicken in every pot" leaves us with longings that gnaw at our souls.

So we keep searching down steamy corridors of sexual experimentation or through elegant halls of cultural sophistication. Some visit the parlor of games and risks, others the smoke-filled rooms of politics and power, still others the classrooms of dialogue and diatribe where we spin philosophies that release us to do whatever we wish.

We walk the paths of leisure and laughter, along the banks of the river called *More,* on to a wall of silver-lined screens where we are titillated, horrified, and desensitized, and into our living rooms where the media moguls shape and mold our perceptions of life, love, and liberty. Yet we keep searching, because we still are empty, and the world around us worse, not better.

What's missing? Interestingly, this new social pilgrimage no longer includes a stop at church. No one asks, "Where is God?" No one ponders that although life was not perfect before we made Him a cultural outcast, at least it was more stable and reliable. Home, school, friendships, and the marketplace, while not always guided by, were at least checked by societal consent to Judeo-Christian values and the good of a higher law.

Hardly anyone seems to reflect on the fact that the major change in these past four decades of increasing complexity and despair has been the systematic dismissal of God from every facet of life and experience. In His place, a host of self-appointed gods has arisen to tell us what is right and wrong in this new world order. And in the streets we hear voices clamoring for societal approval of their right to do as they please without moral judgment or reprisal.

If you wonder why America struggles so today, then think of what happens in a life or in a society when you shut out the One who is truth, wisdom, reality, and hope.

And think of the privilege we have as believers, who, while we may sometimes feel shut out and underclassed, are the presence of God in a land that ignores Him. We can be the fountain of life for those who finally tire of their own ways and come to find Him through us.

We now live in an environment much like that of the first-century church. To those believers, Christ said, "You are the light of the world. A city set on a hill cannot be hidden . . . In the same way, let your light shine before others, so that they may see your good works and give glory to your Father who is in heaven" (Matthew 5:14, 16).

FOLLOWERS ARE LEADERS

You've probably noticed the apparent leadership vacuum in our country.

To hear most people talk, it certainly is true in the world of politics. This current political year is full of skepticism toward government, both national and local. "Whatever happened to the great leaders of the past?" people ask. "Where are the gifted statesmen who can engender the enthusiasm that seems so lacking these days?"

This yawning vacancy of leadership is also evident on the church front. Rarely a week goes by that I don't receive a query from some church that is looking for a pastor. "It sure is tough finding the right man for the job" has become a familiar refrain. As I write this, three major seminaries and one Christian college are searching for a president to carry their banner.

A friend and I were chatting recently about this leadership gap. "Evangelicalism has strong roots in our country," we agreed. "There should be a whole pool of potential leaders. Why is there still so much head-scratching about finding people who are ready to lead?"

While I believe that God sovereignly raises His leaders in His time, this constant concern about leadership indicates that, humanly speaking, we have a crisis.

As I was tossing this problem around in my mind, I found myself wondering if perhaps the problem is not one of leadership, but of followership.

Could it be that we place too much emphasis on creating and grooming leaders, when the vast majority of those who will advance the cause of Christ will be followers? Followers who need not be embarrassed that they are not leaders and who do not need to waste their time aspiring to be leaders.

In a real sense, leaders are born more than they are made. They are born at the right time and place with unique gifts bestowed by our Father in heaven. Every generation has only a handful of truly outstanding leaders.

Given this, we need to rethink our focus on leaders and leadership. Nearly every seminary catalog or college advertisement I see claims that the institution is in the business of producing leaders. I've often felt bad for the vast number of students enrolled in these programs, because most of them never will be, nor were they ever intended to be, great leaders.

God redeemed *all* of us to be *followers* of Him. And He asks us to use our gifts effectively in every context of life. What I love about this perspective is that it involves something each of us can accomplish—the goal of being a "good and faithful" servant, wherever we may be and whatever our situation.

Living in an environment that pushes Christians to expect that somehow we can all become leaders will leave most of us disappointed and discouraged. Living in the context of the scriptural injunctions to be faithful to our gifts and calling, however, is not only achievable, but it can be highly rewarding as well.

The New Testament's injunctions about being an effective follower far outnumber any particular passages that deal with leadership. In fact, the passages that talk about leadership underscore the truth that even those in authority must first be servants and followers of Jesus Christ.

So why don't we hear more discussion about followership? And about creating great followers who are so adept at following Christ that they rise among the masses as credible and effective models of service to the Lord?

When that happens, leaders—without any fanfare or the mastery of sophisticated management techniques—will rise to the top.

Becoming an effective follower will bring to our lives those dynamics that others will want to emulate. In that way, we will quite naturally lead others to desire to become followers of Christ as well.

Those who ultimately lead in the church are those who master an unswerving allegiance to the values and principles of Scripture and commit themselves first and foremost as dedicated followers of Christ.

When I think about those who will ultimately fill the pulpits and presidential chairs in our leading organizations across the land, I find myself praying that somewhere out there, individuals will rise from among us with leadership credentials that are rooted in a life that has so mastered followership that they naturally lead others in their path. That's who I'd look for if I were responsible to fill a vacancy.

Don't be surprised if those who lead us tomorrow will be the ones who have learned to follow Christ today.

WE THE PEOPLE

Once again we are in the midst of a national political campaign that brings democracy to center stage for the entire world to watch. This is democracy in its premiere performance.

Democracy is the rule of the people by representative government for the ultimate benefit of the people. The system would be close to perfect if it weren't *for the people*.

The attempt to govern by and for all the people has divided our nation into competing interests and plunged us into the vortex of division and despair. Baser human instincts, which drive us to put ourselves ahead regardless of others' interests and concerns, have corrupted our democracy. The system is pulled from every side by the passion for power and the protection of conflicting values.

In spite of these self-destroying tendencies that we inflict on our system, democracy remains the best form of government on this planet. Yet we as Christians have to remind ourselves that there is a better system for the governance of our lives.

The day is coming when those who have been drawn by God's love through the passage of redemption will be ruled by a gracious but autocratic dictatorial system. This will forever be the very best and finest form of government. In that glorious day, God will reign in a universe not tainted by self-centered agendas and not threatened by another fall. Sin, death, and hell will enter eternal captivity. We will be locked into righteousness, unable to sin, praising and glorifying an almighty and perfect God to whom we will gladly submit.

Heaven will be an eternal celebration, not of our own significance, but of the significance of our Lord. We will marvel at His wisdom and power. And Scripture has indicated that representatives from every tribe and nation will be brought together. "Red and yellow, black and white," as the song says, will be equally precious in His sight.

In heaven there will be no competition from special interest groups, no conflict of values, no manipulative power plays—none of the things we expect in a political campaign.

During the past few weeks, as the political race in America has intensified, I've realized again that I'm a citizen of a different land, a land where Christ will rule and reign. The New Testament makes it clear that I need to reflect that identity by living by the rules and values of my true home (Philippians 1:21; 3:17–21).

God has called His community here on earth to live like heaven, to look like heaven. This ultimately means that we are dedicated to something far beyond ourselves. Resisting the seduction to advance our own significance and our own agendas, we have the privilege to ensure that love, mercy, grace, kindness, justice, and righteousness reign through us.

When the people of this splintered culture look at us, they should see no one vying for power or advancing personal interests. Instead, they should see a happy equity among the servants of God's agenda.

They should wonder that we use power not for our glory but to empower others for His glory. As they busily scurry to hoard their personal resources for fleeting pleasure, they should marvel that we dedicate our resources for the redemption and restoration of others.

Looking like heaven also means that we heartily welcome to our fellowship people from every tribe and nation—not just with a tip of the hat, but also with a soul embrace of our brotherhood.

We share a mutual calling to something beyond ourselves, something far more significant than the color of our skin or the place of our birth. The church includes Republicans and Democrats, political liberals and conservatives, living, working and loving together as one in Christ. We can and must value each other as equal partners in the outworking of God's redemptive purposes.

There is no place in heaven for the racism and the classism that divide our present political system. Those who have not yet moved through the glorious liberating experience of Christ's cleansing work should wonder when they look at us. How is it that while they strive to keep the lid on smoldering racial tension, God's people have come together as one, enjoying the unique warmth and variety that only diversity can bring?

It would be hard to measure the impact we could make if we went a step beyond democracy and exhibited the best results of what it means to live joyfully under the authority of King Jesus. It would indeed be a bit of heaven on earth.

NOW THAT'S SIGNIFICANT

We hear a lot about the tragedy of addictions in our society. Addictions to food, drugs, alcohol, tobacco, sex, and pornography have given rise to support groups and varied types of therapy to liberate lives from these enslaving habits.

Interestingly, we hear little about an addiction that is common to most of us. This one can be even more debilitating—the addiction to our own significance.

We normally assume that life is driven by the need for success, power, or security. These, however, are merely passageways that lead us to a sense of significance. We all want to believe that we count. To feel insignificant, as if we do not count, is a track toward ultimate despair.

So we live and act to prove that we are significant. We pile up symbols of our significance: houses, cars, careers, where we go on vacation, the people we know, what our business cards say. Inside, pride manages the process by doing everything within its power to maintain, promote, enhance, and protect our personal significance.

The debilitating effect of this addiction is that it creates within us a focus on self that preoccupies our attention and forms the grid through which we make our decisions.

As we look in the rearview mirror of history, there is a profound incident that provides a model for release from this bondage to self and our own significance.

On Palm Sunday, nearly two thousand years ago, an enthusiastic crowd welcomed Jesus Christ to Jerusalem. The coats they laid in His path symbolized submission to His authority. The palm branches signified their acclaim to a conquering hero. To the casual observer, it was a massive celebration of His personal significance.

But a closer look reveals something much different. Heroes normally arrived on powerful stallions. Christ chose to come on a donkey—a symbol of servanthood.

Christ knew that the week ahead would bring Him to the cross. While the crowds hailed His significance, His commitment was to *serve* and *sacrifice* in order to accomplish what was truly significant.

The example of Christ cuts a dramatically new path for us. Society tells us that significant people are not servants—they *have* servants. And those who suffer are weak and powerless—the insignificant in our society.

Yet Jesus Christ "made himself nothing, taking the form of a servant" (Philippians 2:7). He willingly gave up the perks of paradise, identifying with us by climbing into our world. Contrary to the pride that drives our passion for significance, He humbled Himself. He obeyed His Father's will all the way to the cross.

It's in the cross that we find our liberation. When we receive the redemption of His cross, we are restored to unhindered fellowship with God. As such, we are completely significant in Christ. We no longer need to live for significance, because His presence fully satisfies the emptiness in our lives.

Realizing this redemptive reality, we are liberated from the bondage of living for significance. We are freed to serve and sacrifice so that we, like Christ, can know the joy of making a significant contribution to others.

The ramifications of this liberation are indeed profound.

Think of approaching the task of parenting from this point of view. Effective parenting means we climb into our children's world as Christ did into ours. It means we do things that are irrelevant to our own significance—such as playing Chutes and Ladders on the living room floor or showing up at Little League games. It requires a willingness to sacrifice our schedules, plans, and perhaps some extra income. It involves a new goal: to help mold their lives so that God can use them in significant ways.

This new perspective is also the key to our role as husbands. Scripture commands us to love our wives "as Christ loved the church and gave himself up for her" (Ephesians 5:25). While some of us may have married our wives hoping they would enhance our significance, the pattern of Christ changes our agenda. Like Christ, we climb into their world and seek to serve them by meeting their needs—even if that means a measure of personal sacrifice.

This pattern proves equally effective in our relationships with others, in the marketplace, in the church, and in every aspect of our lives.

FAMILY

Our family was just finishing a great few days of vacation in Washington, D.C. As our friends drove us to the airport, the skies opened and a deluge of rain slowed traffic on the interstate to a crawl. Wondering if we would reach the airport in time, we took our bags from the back of the station wagon and held them in our laps, ready to jump out in an instant.

Our friends dropped us off in front of the terminal, and I splashed toward the entrance like a mother duck with her ducklings close behind. At the canopy, I brushed by a man standing directly in our way. As I passed him, I said, "Family coming."

"Big deal!" he muttered.

As I thought back on that hectic rush, I realized that the man's words were a concise statement of our culture's view of family.

Solid families are society's strongest foundation. Yet in the past decades, several forces have been chipping away at it. The desire for things often has drawn both parents into the marketplace, leaving children to be reared in public centers. The drive for self-fulfillment has convinced some parents that divorce will give them "space" to grow.

Feminist rhetoric has convinced many women to delay motherhood and homemaking until later in life and then encourages them to jump back into the marketplace as soon as possible, putting them under the phenomenal stress of trying to be mother, wife, and businessperson.

Many men have accepted the cultural line that the way to success, power, and prestige is to pour themselves into their work instead of giving priority to family. But society's definition of success eventually leaves them empty.

Yet these changing cultural ethics have not created a better society or fostered better people. Quite the opposite. Our nation is struggling with the economic and political weight of these broken pieces of family.

We who follow Christ have a strategic opportunity. Through our families, we can display to the world that Jesus Christ is more than an ethereal religious notion, that He makes a real difference in our homes.

We start by understanding that family is indeed a "big deal" to God. As His first created social structure, it stands as a paramount priority.

Family is where true intimacy develops. Husband and wife step from their aloneness and begin the wonderful adventure toward oneness of mind, heart, spirit, body, and soul.

Family is where couples experience the greatest miracle or existence. From their love springs another life, a combination of their own qualities and yet unique.

Family is where children are sheltered and nurtured. Here they find safety and love, they see truth lived as well as taught, and they develop strength and stability as they move toward independence.

Family is where our children hear about God and have their spiritual lives fashioned and formed.

Family is where we model for the world the picture of Christ and the church, His unconditional love, and our happy submission to Him.

Thankfully, God has not left us without a pattern to follow. Good families result from following the simple, yet profound, principles of Scripture: marriage partners who willingly leave their past and cling to each other; husbands who unselfishly love their wives; wives who graciously cooperate and complement the relationship; fathers who nurture their children in the Lord instead of provoking them to anger; children who obey, honor, and respect their parents (Ephesians 5, 6).

This biblical pattern provides deep joy and satisfaction as we watch our families develop. Even more glorious, we know that it makes our homes stand as a vibrant testimony to the reality of Jesus Christ.

I recall the joy of baptizing a young couple who were led to Christ by their neighbors. "What makes your home so different?" they had asked. When the neighbors explained their commitment to Christ, that night the couple received Him as Savior.

In July, Martie and I had the joy of sitting together while another couple, my son and his beautiful bride, made their promises to each other before God, family, and friends. While it will not always be easy for Joe and Joy, I am thankful that they know the Savior and that they wish to follow His pattern for the family. What a wonderful privilege to have a home where love, joy, and peace are the predominant commodities.

The sassafras is a small tree, native to Michigan, from whose roots come the extract for root beer. I still remember the first time my dad broke a root to let me smell the familiar aroma. He pointed out the unusual pattern of the leaves—the three different-shaped leaves. Those three different leaves are found on every sassafras, everywhere, every time.

It's no mistake. It's one of the marvels of a world created not by chance, but by an intelligent Creator who left His fingerprints all around—traces of the unusual to catch our attention and draw our eyes to Him.

God seeks to be known. He has left signs of His presence everywhere.

- In the heavens: "The heavens declare the glory of God, and the sky above proclaims his handiwork" (Psalm 19:1).
- In the life of Christ: "The Word became flesh and dwelt among us, and we have seen his glory, glory as of the only Son from the Father, full of grace and truth" (John 1:14).
- In His creation on land and sea: "The earth is the Lord's and the fullness thereof, the world and those who dwell therein, for he has founded it upon the seas and established it upon the rivers"(Psalm 24:1).

Wherever we look, His existence and glory are clearly displayed.

March is the month the humpback whales wind up their calving season in the warm waters of Maui, Hawaii, and begin their trek back to Alaska to feed through the summer.

These mysterious creatures are a marvelous piece of God's handiwork. As I listened this past winter to a naturalist explain their unique habits, my heart grew quiet with a sense of awe toward God the creator.

Ranging from forty to forty-five feet long, the adult weighs about a ton per foot and carries another one thousand pounds of barnacles.

When they arrive in the Islands each year, the humpbacks go to the same place—a territory staked out for their families. They calve in the sheltered coves, away from predator sharks that would eat their young.

Babies are born breech so that these newborn mammals will immediately head for the surface to gulp their first breath of air. The process is aided by another humpback that plays the role of mid-wife, pushing the baby—all five to nine tons—to its air supply.

Periodically the whales leap from the water, extending their full frame into the air. The splash from their freefall back into the ocean is visible up to four miles away. The air they exhaust through their spout is released at a velocity of three hundred miles per hour.

Most intriguing, however, is their song. Humpbacks sing a song of patterned noises that can travel more than fifty miles under water. Every humpback sings the same song, and each year the song changes slightly.

All humpbacks sing the modified version uniformly, whether in the Atlantic or Pacific. After a few years, an entirely new song is sung.

The naturalist's closing statement interrupted my thoughts of the wonder and glory of God revealed in these animals: "If you had been here forty to fifty million years ago, you would not have seen these whales, because they evolved from land mammals."

I pondered the statement for a moment. *How would that happen?* I wondered. *Did some four-footed beast live in the shallow surf for millions of years until all the apparatus was in place to swim into the deep?*

It seemed incredible to imagine that the sophisticated and intelligent design of the humpback could have come about by chance and a statistical improbability that a land animal could change so dramatically.

Beyond that, however, my heart sank to think that in one moment that comment had stripped God of the glory and honor due His name.

Of all the effects that evolutionistic theory has had on the values and mores of our culture, the worst is that it has misattributed to mere chance the fingerprints of God on all that is around us. Is it any wonder that modern man doubts the existence of God and scoffs at His relevance?

Paul's words in Romans 1:18–20 bring a sober warning: "The wrath of God is revealed from heaven against all ungodliness and unrighteousness of men, who by their unrighteousness suppress the truth. For what can be known about God is plain to them, because God has shown it to them. For his invisible attributes, namely, his eternal power and divine nature, have been clearly perceived, ever since the creation of the world, in the things that have been made. So they are without excuse."

We who have been redeemed are redeemed to glorify God (1 Corinthians 6:19–20). Yet I wonder how often we rob God, instead, of the evidence of His presence. I wonder if others see some of Him when they see me.

PART TWO

HAVING PUT ON THE BREASTPLATE OF RIGHTEOUSNESS

BLESS THE BOUNDARIES

Boundaries are out of bounds. In a day when personal freedom is celebrated as an inalienable right, any talk of lifestyle restriction is viewed as an infringement on sacred territory. As long as you don't hurt anyone else, your options are limitless. In case you haven't recognized this addiction to having life our own way, consider the way we sell our products.

Advertisers spend millions to understand what people want and then to appeal to their desires. The concept of moral restraint is obviously out of favor when Nike sells shoes with a slogan like "Just Do It" and Burger King trumpets, "Sometimes you gotta break the rules." A liquor company markets the notion, "Some people embrace the night because rules of the day do not apply." Easy Spirit shoes "conform to your foot so you don't have to conform to anything." Even Merrill Lynch declares, "Your world should know no boundaries."

In all of this there is a glaring inconsistency. Personal morality is the only place where we are encouraged to believe "boundaryless" living is a worthy goal. Our society erects boundaries throughout its structure.

Communities post speed limits and take pains to enforce them. Health experts increasingly tell us we must restrict our diets or face serious medical consequences. We raise our children with strict boundaries. Things like not crossing the street alone and not being friendly to strangers are all viewed as commonsense restrictions. Businesses have dress codes, and the marketplace has its own code of ethics that must not be violated.

In fact, the refusal to apply boundaries to personal behavior is a cultural boundary in itself. Anyone who aggressively speaks out against it is considered out of bounds.

What no one seems to notice is that the more we encourage living life by unbridled instincts, the more our society is marked by a gnawing sense of meaninglessness, distress, and despair. Robert Bork underscores this in his book, *Slouching Towards Gomorrah*. He writes, "Our modern, virtually unqualified, enthusiasm for liberty forgets that liberty can only be 'the space between the walls,' the walls of morality and law based upon morality. It is sensible to argue about how far apart the walls should be set, but it is cultural suicide to demand all space and no walls."

Bork must have read the proverb, "There is a way that seems right to a man, but its end is the way to death" (Proverbs 14:12).

Isn't it interesting that Eve didn't know shame and alienation until she believed the adversary who called God's boundaries into question (Genesis 3:1–6)? In all the years that I have worked with people, I have yet to meet one whose life was in disarray because he had been faithful to God's parameters. Humpty-Dumpty lives are shattered by the consequences of a decision to test the edge of the boundaries.

God's people should have a distinctly different view of boundaries. Those of us who trust in God refuse to believe that boundaries are God's way of taking the pizzazz out of life. We know that His boundaries are actually fences constructed with wisdom, love, and mercy at the sane perimeter of life to help us avoid the treachery of our naiveté.

I love the psalmist's perspective when he affirms that the truly blessed person is the one whose "delight is in the law of the Lord, and on his law he meditates day and night." He goes on to describe the one who celebrates the boundaries as one who is "like a tree planted by streams of water that yields its fruit in its season, and its leaf does not wither. In all that he does, he prospers" (Psalm 1:2–3).

In Psalm 119 you can almost feel the exuberant affection the writer has for God's boundaries. "O how I love your law! It is my meditation all the day . . . How sweet are your words to my taste, sweeter than honey to my mouth! . . . Your word is a lamp to my feet and a light to my path . . . I incline my heart to perform your statutes forever, to the end (vv. 97, 103, 105, 112).

While our world curses the boundaries, the truly free know better—they bless the boundaries.

SEEING BEYOND THE STYLE

In case you haven't noticed, we live in a style-over-substance world. In many respects, imaging, glitz, and glamour have become more important than truth and content. It's the *packaging* of our products, personalities, and politicians that matters most.

Even a casual glance at today's church reveals that we Christians have not escaped the pressure to elevate the importance of style. In fact, our most heated discussions and divisions frequently originate with issues of style rather than substance.

We should, of course, commit ourselves to doing things well. The nature of Christ as creator demands that we do His work with excellence. Furthermore, in a world that spends millions to project compelling images, we can hardly get away with doing things in a shabby, stodgy style and still hope to attract people to Christ.

What concerns me, however, is that so much of our clamoring and consternation focuses on style. Not necessarily on whether we do God's work with style, but rather the *kind* of style we use. Worse yet, we tend to ascribe spiritual values to the styles we prefer.

This is particularly true regarding styles of worship.

I'm reminded of a wonderful Sunday morning experience I enjoyed at the House of the Lord in Akron, Ohio. This church is predominantly black, both in its constituency and its worship style. It was a thrill to see such spontaneous joy, energy, and authentic celebration sincerely presented to the Lord. Make no mistake, these brothers and sisters have not lost the joy!

The service also had substance. For example, the choir members did a rousing rendition of "The Hallelujah Chorus"—in their style.

Earlier in the morning, however, I was equally impressed with a far different experience. As I was getting ready to go to church, I happened on a live telecast of an Anglican worship service from St. Paul's Cathedral in London. The service was commemorating the victory in World War II.

I was struck with the power and grandeur of the liturgy and the music. The Scripture readings focused my thoughts on the almighty, sovereign, omnipotent God. The music was rich and brilliant, as herald trumpets, choirs, and the congregation resounded with praise. All of it fit traditional and classical forms of expression. Though the service was thousands of miles away, I found my heart drawn close to God.

The experience was far different from the worship service I would soon attend at the House of the Lord in Akron. There was a dramatic difference in style, but the substance was the same.

In congregations across our land, we see an increasing multiplicity of worship styles. In part, this reflects the shifting culture. Younger generations relate to music and worship styles that differ from what earlier generations are accustomed to. Our temptation is to attach spiritual meaning to styles and to forget that the substance of worship, not the style, is what interests God.

I doubt if it makes much difference to God whether the choir sways or herald trumpets play from the balconies of a cathedral. What He does care about is that we worship in spirit and in truth—"for the Father is seeking such people to worship him" (John 4:23).

He cares that we honor Him with our hearts, and not just our lips (Matthew 15:8). He cares that we worship Him with thankfulness, good deeds, and a generous spirit (Hebrews 13:15–16).

Those of us who worship in forms that are more structured and staid must do so from spirits that are acceptable to God. And those of us who relate to more contemporary, spontaneous, and expressive styles of worship must remember that we are not necessarily more acceptable to God. We must be sure our forms accurately reflect truth and that they are not merely ways of seeking our own emotional therapy.

"Boomers" and "Busters" shouldn't write off more traditional worship styles. Substance is the issue.

Nor should we old-timers dismiss the newer forms. Substance is the issue. Worship is measured by its conformity both to the truth and to the spirit in which it is done.

Let's remember that in worship, God is measuring our hearts. He is listening for echoes of truth to fill His throne room so that His pleasure might be full.

WITH RUNNER'S EYES

A few weeks ago I sat on the platform of the historic Torrey-Gray auditorium on our campus, struck by the scene of nearly five hundred graduates before me from our undergraduate, graduate, and external studies divisions. For most of them, the ceremony was like the firing of the starter's gun. With an intensive season of training behind them, these graduates were now beginning a life of ministry.

I thought of what the writer to the Hebrews said: "Therefore, since we are surrounded by so great a cloud of witnesses, let us also lay aside every weight, and sin which clings so closely, and let us run with endurance the race that is set before us" (12:1).

Though every Christian is called to run this race, the marathon of vocational ministry is especially challenging. Often it feels like an obstacle course. Our graduates will at times be unheralded and unheeded; they may feel underpaid, under-loved, and under-affirmed.

Of all the temptations they face, the most deadly seduction will be to compare themselves with those who are off the track. Often it is the unrighteous, unfaithful, and ungodly that prosper in this world. Those in ministry may wonder, *Why should I live with grief when so many others get the gain?*

This was the near downfall of Asaph. In Psalm 73 he admitted, "My feet had almost stumbled, my steps had nearly slipped. For I was envious of the arrogant when I saw the prosperity of the wicked" (vv. 2–3). The success of proud and godless people had plunged Asaph into deep despair. "All in vain have I kept my heart clean," he complained, "and washed my hands in innocence. For all the day long I have been stricken and rebuked every morning" (vv. 13–14).

Asaph had served what he thought was a loving and a good God. Now his calling seemed a cashless, comfortless arrangement. What had begun as heartfelt devotion now declined into a threatening depression.

The truth that Asaph affirmed at the beginning of his psalm—"Truly God is good to Israel, to those who are pure in heart" (v. 1)—was in tension with his perception. But the tension faded when he "went into the sanctuary of God" (v. 17).

How dramatically different our life appears when seen from God's point of view! Asaph admitted that he had made a terrible mistake in even thinking about trading places with the unfaithful. Once he entered God's sanctuary, he "discerned their end" (v. 17).

At that point Asaph realized that momentary prosperity has no value in terms of eternal accountability before a righteous and holy God. As our Lord reminded us, "What will it profit a man if he gains the whole world and forfeits his life? Or what shall a man give in return for his life?" (Matthew 16:26).

Someone once stated that if all you have in eternity is hell, then the only heaven you will ever know is on this earth. If you spend eternity in heaven, however, then the only hell you will ever know is on earth.

Once we see life in the perspective of eternal reality and leave our fallen perceptual fantasies, it is amazing how the windows of truth open for us. Asaph confessed to God, "When my soul was embittered, when I was pricked in heart, I was brutish and ignorant; I was like a beast toward you" (Psalm 73:21–22).

He then began to revel in the rewards of the righteous. Rewards that far transcend either cash or comfort. "Nevertheless, I am continually with you; you hold my right hand. You guide me with your counsel, and afterward you will receive me to glory" (vv. 23–24).

Those who are God's will enjoy His presence, His protection, His wise guidance through the maze of life, and the assurance that He will receive us home to an eternity of fulfilled joy and pleasure with Him.

Having resolved the tension between his perception and the truth, Asaph exclaims, "Whom have I in heaven but you? And there is nothing on earth that I desire besides you" (v. 25).

Not only graduates, but also all of us who are committed to a life of non-negotiated service to God, may be tempted to leave the race for short-term gain. Yet to run successfully, we must "[look] to Jesus, the founder and perfecter of our faith, who for the joy that was set before him endured the cross" (Hebrews 12:2).

As runners, we know that no matter how hard the course, it will be worth it all when we snap the tape and find ourselves home. Particularly if we hear Him say, "Well done, good and faithful servant."

MURPHY'S LAW

If you've never heard of Murphy's Law, you've certainly experienced it. According to Murphy's maxim, "If anything can go wrong, it will." I have a friend who says that there is a law that supersedes Murphy's—known as O'Toole's Law—which states that Murphy was an optimist.

For those of us who keep expecting that this world will be a source for peace and positive prospects, we live in continuous states of disappointment.

Murphy may have been a theologian. Or at least he may have known what Christ said in John 16:33, that "in the world you will have tribulation." When John spoke of the world, he was speaking of the disordered, dysfunctional sphere of existence that is manipulated by Satan.

Reflecting on the day that everything changed helps us understand why this world provides such a painful experience.

Genesis tells us that God created a world of magnificent order in six days. He made a man and woman, put them in charge of the material order, and provided unhindered relationship with Himself.

But then, everything changed! Adam and Eve succumbed to Satan's seduction. At that point, the world and all of its inhabitants fell into the grip of sin. The result was disorder and dysfunction.

When Christ reminds us that we should expect trouble from this fallen world, we might remind ourselves that trouble is sometimes just the stuff that happens. Lost keys and fender-bender days when, no matter how we try, nothing goes right.

Sometimes the trouble in this world is because we live not only in a fallen environment, but also in a world full of disordered and dysfunctional people. We've become victimized by their selfishness, greed, lust, and insensitivity.

Frankly, we must remember that sometimes the trouble we experience comes from the fact that you and I are fallen. In the words of Pogo, "We have met the enemy, and he is us."

And there is the trouble of living in an increasingly disordered, dysfunctional society that for the past forty years has been drumming God out of His proper place. More and more, as Christ said, the world will hate us because it hated Him (John 15:18–19). There's no doubt we are in for more disquieting experiences with the world as our claims of the reality of God, the uniqueness of Christ, and the existence of absolutes will seem even more outdated. We will increasingly be seen and treated as outcasts in this world.

This world is trouble looking for a place to happen. And while there will always be some good, it cannot be attributed to this world's system, but rather to its conformity to God's design.

Given this theological verification of both Murphy and O'Toole, can we ever expect any measure of peace? Yes!

Because in the same verse that Christ warned that *in this world* we would have trouble, He also welcomed us to live *in Him*. He told His disciples, "In me you may have peace" (John 16:33).

The peace is rooted in the realities of the things that Christ had just told the disciples. He gave them five resources for peace: their love for one another, the assurance of His coming to take them to heaven, the provision of the indwelling Holy Spirit, the wonderful privilege of abiding in Him, and the opportunity for prayer to receive what they needed.

We can possess peace in this world only through Christ. But that fact makes none of us exempt from this world's pain and trauma.

Christ assured us that while He would give us peace in the midst of the world's pain, He also would be the source for our courage and confidence because, "I have overcome the world."

Interestingly, the word *overcome* carries the nuance of a past event that has a continuing effect. Not only has He conquered the fallen world system through His death and resurrection, but also He continues to provide victory for all who will find it in Him.

The believer's hope and confidence is that no matter how tough times get here, Christ's overcoming power guarantees that in all things God works for the good (Romans 8:28).

I'm convinced as I study Scripture that He never wastes His servants. Those of us who look to Him will find ultimate glory on the other side of any pain that this world might inflict upon us.

I don't know what you expect from this world, but if you're looking for peace in life, it is found only in Christ.

While this world is our place, He is our passion. In Him, we have peace. As He said, "Take heart! I have overcome the world."

WHAT MIGHT HAVE BEEN

Thanksgiving has always been my favorite holiday. It seems so warm, so uncluttered, so family oriented. It's the holiday that commercialism forgot.

But, given my love for the day, it has brought some challenges. Particularly when the family took turns around the table, each telling what we were thankful for. What I said seemed so routine, average, unspectacular.

For some reason, God chose to put me in a good family with good parents. He has provided for all of my needs and many of my desires. He redeemed me when I was a young boy, so my list of blessings seems a lot like other people's lists.

Over the years, I've come to appreciate more deeply those "ordinary" items on my list. I know that many people never had the security of a healthy family. Living in Chicago, I'm very aware of those who have little of this world's provision and must beg and scrape for what they need. And as I've grown to understand more fully the consequence of sin, I'm saddened by the fact that the vast majority of those I pass every day have no assurance of escaping the fair and just judgment of God for sin.

I've come to realize that if Christ does nothing more than redeem me, He's already done far more than I deserve. Simply by canceling hell and guaranteeing heaven, He has given plenty of reasons for heartfelt thanks.

Recently, however, I've added another category to my list of things to be thankful for. It's the category of being grateful to God for sparing me from what might have been.

While studying the plight of Job, I noticed that God stood as the sovereign sentinel at the gate of his life, letting in only what could be used for ultimate gain and glory. I realized that God also keeps many things out of my life every day that I don't see.

First Corinthians 10:13 makes it clear that God will not permit trials beyond what we are able to bear. For most of us, our days are rather routine, with no observable sovereign interventions for which we can give stellar testimony. But I've come to realize that every night when I lay my head on the pillow, I can thank God for keeping out those things that would destroy and undo me.

The most recent item on my list, in this category of praising God for what might have been, occurred to me soon after last year's Founder's Week, an annual Bible conference sponsored by Moody Bible Institute. I was reflecting on the marvelous afternoon when the Brooklyn Tabernacle Choir led us in worship.

The visual impact alone was stunning: 180 black, Hispanic, and white faces singing praise for the redemptive work of God. What struck me about this choir, which does not hire professionals, were the tears running down the singers' faces. These people, many of whom were saved from the depths of despair, were obviously grateful that God had redeemed, transformed, and given them a new eternal lease on life.

Redemption, though appreciated, rarely seemed that gripping in my soul, I realized. Because I was saved early in life, the only redemptive release I experienced was deliverance from things like biting my sister.

Then it struck me. I had never really stopped to understand redemption in terms of what might have been. As this idea unfolded in my heart and mind, I thought about what my life might be like today if it weren't for the fact that God had redeemed me.

I'm a rather compulsive, spontaneous person. I might be a chain smoker, perhaps even an alcoholic. I wondered where self-centeredness would have taken me in terms of shattered relationships and loss of fulfillment if it had not been for the balancing tension of the Spirit in my life.

I wondered how many marriages I might have gone through or what I might have done to my children, had it not been for the love of Christ that has changed and filled my life, enabling me to love others in some measure the way that He has loved me.

I found myself wondering where my greed or lusts might have taken me. Down what kind of dead-end streets, with shame and despair as the ultimate reward of pleasing basic passions.

As I was considering these thoughts, my soul was gripped with a fresh sense of gratitude to God for the fact that He has redeemed me. For me, the testimony of redemption is rejoicing about being unscarred from what might have been.

All of this to say that Thanksgiving has become even more special for me. I have learned a new dimension to giving thanks in everything. To give thanks for those things from which I have been sovereignly spared.

THE MAKING OF A MAN

I was born male. But early in my life, I learned that being male did not necessarily make me a man.

I realized this the first time somebody said, "Joe, be a man." It was probably when I had started crying or refused to eat my spinach. I discovered that I had a new task in life: to go beyond just being a male and discover what it meant to be a "man."

That agenda became more urgent as I grew through adolescence. Being a man meant to be tough and athletic. It meant never saying I was sorry or admitting that I was wrong. Real men don't cry, I learned. They woo women, work hard, and win. A host of other cultural expectations whiplashed me from one side of the landscape to the other.

Even today, as a man nearing the mid-century mark, I find that the task of manhood is as challenging and confusing as ever.

What does it mean to be a man? Society presents us with the macho Marlboro man, the mild-mannered sensitive man, the suave artsy man, the Monday night football man, and the cunning marketplace man who moves through the corporate stream like a shark.

These contrasting portraits make many of us feel insecure about our manhood. There always seems to be a better athlete or a more successful businessman. There is always someone who is slimmer, trimmer, and tougher than we are.

When women reject us, these insecurities surface painfully. (Remember how you felt when the first girl you asked out said no?) When confronted by family pressures or marketplace sharks, we feel intimidated. Our cultural environment compounds the problem, making some of us feel almost ashamed of our masculinity.

One of the many things I love about my personal relationship with Jesus Christ is that He cuts through all the cultural confusion and leads me to a focused, singular agenda of true manhood. This agenda doesn't necessarily lead us men to society's definition of success. But it does bring great significance. At the end of life, we can look back through the rearview mirror and see that we have left a legacy of significance and worth through our family, our children, our relationships to others, our relationships to society, and our investments for God.

The incredible reality is that Jesus Christ dwells within all of us who have come to His cross and tasted the new wine of redemption. His redemptive purpose for us on this planet is that we cultivate a relationship with Him so strong and deep that He emerges through all that we are. In this way the world will see not only our changed life but also the glory of His character in all aspects of our existence.

And there is the key!

It is our privilege as redeemed men to allow Christ to emerge through us, through the particular qualities we have as men.

But many of us fear that. We're afraid that if we fully yield the reins of our life to Christ, He will take away our manhood. Victims of a demasculinized portrait of Christ, we have forgotten that His perfect blend of divinity and humanity was expressed through His existence as a man. He was the perfect expression of manhood. While that meant He had a special compassionate side, He also displayed strength and power—enough strength and power to attract strong men as His followers. Enough so that they even gave up their careers and personal ambitions and followed Him.

Jesus Christ does not at all diminish our manhood. He emerges through the distinct qualities of our maleness to create a fuller and richer expression of what a man can be.

He redefines our manhood by replacing the motivations of the world with new guidelines for success. He directs our manhood along the path of ultimate significance. He takes our instincts to protect, provide, conquer, and accumulate, and points them in productive directions.

In the expression of our manhood, He becomes the central control system of our life that dictates all that we do, all that we are, and all that we hope to become.

As the apostle Paul wrote, "It is God who works in you, both to will and to work for his good purpose" (Philippians 2:13). Our goal, he explained, is to stretch toward "the measure of the stature of the fullness of Christ" (Ephesians 4:13). That maturity, when expressed distinctively by men, will keep us from being whiplashed by our culture, "tossed to and fro by the waves and carried about by every wind of doctrine" (Ephesians 4:14).

When we tell our boys to "be a man," they need to know how that can happen— through the emergence of the indwelling Christ.

If you know baseball, you probably know about Ernie Harwell. For decades, Ernie has been the voice of the Detroit Tigers. He knows more trivia and interesting baseball stories than a dozen experts put together. His colorful, down-home commentaries are so good that many people turn down the sound on their television and turn up Ernie on the radio as they watch the game.

Ernie is one of only three baseball announcers to be named to the Baseball Hall of Fame and the only announcer to have been traded for a player.

What is most significant, however, is his deep commitment to the Lord Jesus Christ. He and his wife have often hosted Bible studies for professional ballplayers. Throughout his life he has proven himself to be a man of integrity and honor.

Given all this, you can imagine the public outcry when the Tiger organization announced that it would not renew Ernie's contract at the end of this season. Though he is 72, Harwell enjoys the overwhelming support of fans. They thought he should stay until the time was right for retirement.

Newspapers across the country carried Ernie's story. "Gentleman Wronged," cried a front-page headline in one Detroit paper. Bumper stickers and radio talk shows voiced the protest. When the Tigers played their first game in Chicago, a plane flew over Comiskey Park with a banner declaring, "Bring Ernie Back."

What most people didn't know is that when Ernie received his pink slip, his wife, Lulu, had just been diagnosed with cancer.

In a press conference, Ernie was asked if he was bitter about his job situation. "Bitter?" he replied. "The Lord's been too good to this tongue-tied boy from Georgia for too many years for me to be bitter."

In my view, this was Ernie's finest moment. The true measure of a man comes when all the chips are down. When we who claim Christ as Lord go through deep waters, we have our greatest opportunity to demonstrate that Christ is sufficient for all of life—for the bad times as well as the good.

What do we do when, living in this fallen place in the midst of a fallen race, we suddenly discover that our world has fallen in on us? We have several choices:

Wallow in the perspective that life is unfair and that people have been unjust.

Internalize blame and guilt.

Lash out at those who caused our pain.

Withdraw into self-pity, assuming the posture of a martyr.

Creatively design ways to get back at those responsible for unraveling our life.

Or, we can turn our faces to our Father in heaven and trust that when He said, "All things work together for good," He meant it (Romans 8:28). We can cling to the reality that God will use our trouble to make us competent and usable (James 1:2–4).

God's agenda for our lives may be far different from our own. He cares more about our character than our convenience, comfort, or cash (Romans 8:28–29). He is more concerned that we become like His Son than that we gain positions of power and prestige (1 Corinthians 6:19–20). He is more interested in the advance of His eternal kingdom than in our accumulation of temporary, earthly possessions (Matthew 6:33).

God intends that we use the trouble in our lives to display His glory. When the disciples saw the man born blind, they were curious (John 9). "Whose sin caused this?" they asked. "Was it the parents' sin or the man's sin while he was in his mother's womb?"

Christ broadened their horizons, declaring that the man had been born for a strategic purpose—to display the glory of God in a disbelieving world.

Christ then healed the man, not only so he could see but also so the world could see the power and the presence of God. It is a wonderful privilege to be a stage on which God's glory is clearly seen.

While troubles are intended for our growth and God's glory, Scripture also assures us that they are accompanied by His sufficient grace, that we might find help in time of need (2 Corinthians 12:9; Hebrews 4:15–16). As we respond to trouble by accepting God's agendas of growth and glory, we can count on the fact that He will indeed give grace to the humble (1 Peter 5:5).

Ernie Harwell is a true hero. There aren't many left. He has done well in good times, and now he has done even better in tough times. Thanks, Ernie, for bringing us the pleasure of good baseball and, more important, for being an all-star, authentic Christian whose heart is fixed on growth and the glory of God.

NOT A VICTIMLESS CRIME

One of the intriguing features of television is the creativity of its ads. I pay attention to advertisements, not just to laugh or to marvel at marketing genius, but because they usually focus on basic desires and interests. The way Madison Avenue appeals to us says a lot about where we are as a culture.

Rarely does an ad make me want to weep; yet recently I watched one with tragic implications. It shows an elderly couple sitting on a front porch swing. As the footage rolls, the wife begins to fantasize. She dreams of dancing the night away on a luxurious cruise ship. The camera then refocuses, showing the couple back on the swing.

Quickly, the ad shifts to a man standing on a street corner. As he waits for a bus, he fantasizes about buying his own car. Next we see him beside a shiny automobile, touching it admiringly. The camera then takes us back to the bus stop, where the man is left standing with his dream, obviously too poor to afford his own transportation.

To this point, I had no idea what the ad was trying to market. Then, in the closing seconds, it showed these words above an overflowing pot of gold: *Illinois State Lottery.*

The message was penetrating and clear: The way to fulfill our dreams is to give up what we have for something we will probably never win. It is tragic enough that a state encourages risking precious resources through gambling. Worse, however, is that this ad appeals to the people who can least afford to risk the few resources they have—the elderly and poor.

To my mind, an ad that plays on the vulnerability of the less fortunate is socially obscene. It victimizes those who are struggling and offers them a hope that is statistically improbable. Hoping against hope, people waste their precious resources and wind up worse off in the end.

The greed of the Illinois Lottery officials who pack the coffers of their lottery fund at the expense of these vulnerable people is not a victimless crime.

The lottery ad was still fresh in my mind when I picked up a paper and read about the marketing of a new cigarette from the R. J. Reynolds Company. "Dakota" is intended to appeal to young "virile females" who like to run with their boyfriends and do what the guys are doing.

The tobacco people know that smoking is addictive and often fatal. Yet when their research shows that these young women are especially prone to start smoking, they point the poison at their prey.

All this for profit. For bottom line. For gain. Is revenue more important than caring for other people's welfare? The company sought out the most vulnerable in society and intentionally marketed an addictive, destructive product toward them.

While the blatant greed-driven behavior of our culture is appalling, the same tendencies often display themselves among those of us who claim to belong to another kingdom.

Think of how often our greed has robbed eternity. We spend so much of our time and money accumulating things "that moth and rust destroy" that we have few resources and little time left to invest in commodities that last forever. This greed victimizes our privilege of seeking first the kingdom of God (Luke 12:31).

Think of how greed tarnishes the testimony of Christ when we as business professionals compromise integrity and biblical values to cut a less than honorable deal.

Or of how greed shreds families when parents devote their best energies to dreams of an extra car, a nicer home, or a better vacation, leaving little strength for rearing children in "the discipline and instruction of the Lord" (Ephesians 6:4).

We are not exempt from the consequences of our own forms of greed. It litters the landscape around us with victims of our self-centered drives. Greed contradicts love. It has no regard for values. It gobbles up all that is ultimately precious in life.

No wonder Christ told us, "Take care, and be on your guard against all covetousness, for one's life does not consist in the abundance of his possessions" (Luke 12:15).

It's not easy to think right in this world gone so wrong. Yet we start by remembering how much we already possess. To have Christ is to have it all! He will never leave us or forsake us. With that truth firmly in hand, we can keep our lives "free from love of money, and be content with what you have" (Hebrews 13:5), liberating ourselves to place loving and caring for Christ, His kingdom, and others above personal gain.

FREEDOM, THE OLD-FASHIONED WAY

Born free? Not really.

Actually, nothing could be further from the truth. We come into this world dependent and limited. Not one of us was exempt from the need to be carried, fed, clothed, changed, and guided.

Yet our need for independence emerges early. Children are soon eager to walk, talk, bathe, and dress themselves and leave the diaper stage—all steps to independence and self-determination.

From season to season, year to year, life is a pilgrimage—a yearning for greater freedom. We go off to school, then to college, and then to a home of our own. At each stage we seek freedom from the restrictions of the past and push toward the time of life that seems to promise ultimate freedom: retirement.

Ironically, each phase of life has limitations and dependencies that prohibit total independence. Parents, teachers, spouses, children, employers, and economic and social restrictions all interfere and cramp our style. Even in retirement, when we imagine we finally will be completely free, the body rebels and we suffer the limitations of age.

Perhaps more disturbing than man's search for unbridled freedom is his insistence on "doing what *I* want to do."

Doing what I want has brought me more trouble than I care to remember. As I grew up, self-determination put me in tension with my parents. During my school years, it put me at odds with my teachers.

Even now, as a husband and father, I find that an occasional lapse into independence can bring disappointments in my relationships with my wife and children.

Our culture unrepentantly defines freedom as "doing things my way." Yet in truth, freedom to do whatever we want is the beginning of bondage.

Unrestrained behavior eventually brings painful consequences and guilt. Alcohol and drug abuse grow out of the philosophy that freedom is the release from all restrictions. Unrestrained sexual behavior, encouraged under the guise of freedom, leads to AIDS and other diseases.

Unchecked behavior has broken homes and shredded relationships, many beyond repair.

Freedom that leads to bondage is no freedom at all. Freedom that results in disease, destruction, and despair is a poor alternative to the freedom available in Christ.

Scripture validates the pursuit of freedom. Yet it directs that pursuit in a manner foreign to our inclinations. Christ says true freedom begins with restrictions.

We find this surprising definition of freedom in John 8:31–32, where Christ says, "If you abide in my word, you are truly my disciples, and you will know the truth, and the truth will set you free."

Notice the sequence. Freedom is not the starting point. Freedom is not my inalienable right. Freedom is, rather, the result of my holding to Christ's teaching, of restricting my life to that which is right and true.

Restricting my life to that which is true sets me free not only from the bondage of addiction and destructive behavior, but free to know unhindered joy, a clear conscience, growing relationships, and life at its fullest.

When I limit myself to honest, biblical business deals, I am free to enjoy a clear conscience, without the haunting fear of getting caught at something unethical.

When I restrict my freedom of choice and practice biblical patterns of parenting, I am free to enjoy my children and am released from destructive patterns that can damage precious relationships.

When I resist the temptation to do whatever I want and limit myself to meeting my wife's needs and bringing happiness to her, I set our relationship free for growth, intimacy, and long-lasting reward.

The Statue of Liberty, a symbol of freedom to millions of immigrants to America, holds a tablet in one hand and a torch high in the other. Apart from the torch of truth, there is no freedom. Freedom is a result of hard, unflinching commitments to those things that come from God's Word of righteousness.

Freedom is not a right with which we are born. It is a God-given privilege realized only as a result of righteous living. It comes the old-fashioned way—we earn it with an undaunted commitment to truth.

"If the Son sets you free, you will be free indeed" (John 8:36).

PART THREE

AS SHOES FOR YOUR FEET...THE GOSPEL OF PEACE

I n the 1990s, Secretary of the Treasury Robert Rubin and his colleague, Alan Greenspan, guided our nation's economy for nearly a decade of breathtaking, wallet-ripping growth. Unprecedented in its upward mobility and enduring tenure, the economy was strong enough to save President Clinton's job and to enrich every American who had access to its spigot. It's that access that makes me wonder.

The economies of our own lives are not as public, nor nearly as complex, as government budgets. We alone control what we do with the resources God has entrusted to our care. We make all the decisions about how and where they are allocated.

In turn, we are also responsible for the economy of the kingdom of Christ. His economy translates into ministry budgets in churches, support for missionaries, funds dispersed to the disadvantaged, pastors who are well cared for, widows who are blessed—and the list goes on.

Because we control the outflow of our personal prosperity, you would think that times of prosperity would be financially prosperous days for the kingdom of Christ. No more wondering where the next dollar is going to come from to get God's work done. No more passionate, embarrassing pleas for God's people to loosen up and love the work of Christ with their checkbooks.

Walking through an inner-city school in Chicago during those times of national prosperity, I was taken by the smiling, energetic faces of kids who were out-performing their public school counterparts by several grade levels. Though they quoted Scripture as if they loved it, those kids were still at risk. Most were fatherless. Many of their older brothers sold drugs on street corners and ruled the neighborhood by gang law. But these kids had a chance. They were embraced by Christ's love at this private Christian school. What does this have to do with prosperous times? Everything.

The school was not sure it could add the next grade because most of its budget came from donations. Parents in this neighborhood had hardly enough money for their next meal. Within twenty-five miles of the Circle Urban Christian School were communities full of Christians taking deep gulps at the spigot of our nation's prosperity. Could it be possible that more of the "good times" money controlled by Christians was going to cars, castles, and mutual funds than to seizing the moment to advance the cause of Christ?

When Paul taught the church at Corinth about giving, he instructed them to give weekly as they had been prospered to help with the work of ministry (1 Corinthians16: 2). It's not that we can't enjoy some of the fruit of our new prosperity (1 Timothy 6:17), but if our hearts beat with Christ's, we will love to invest in things that thieves cannot steal (Luke 12:31–34).

Economic good times can be tough times to do good for Christ. In bad times, we get really serious about doing what is right for Him. We can't afford to lose His blessing. But when He blesses us abundantly, we are prone to forget Him (Deuteronomy 6:10–12). A season of unparalleled economic growth is our opportunity to express our love to Him by giving to the worthy enterprise of His work.

Robert Rubin had a sign on his desk that read, "The Buck Starts Here." The buck starts here for us as well. I wonder if it has ever crossed our minds that God may permit robust economies to underwrite a more robust economy for the kingdom.

UNHERALDED HERO

Does the name *Josh Gibson* ring a bell?

In a world short on heroes, baseball served up a home-run competition in the fall of 1998 that pitted muscleman Mark McGwire against the affable gentleman Sammy Sosa. All of America watched as the two vied day after day to break one of sports' most coveted records. They both surpassed Babe Ruth's sixty homeruns and then flew by Roger Maris's claim of sixty-one before McGwire pulled away and took the prize with seventy homers.

Enter Mr. Gibson. In all of the hullabaloo over the Sosa-McGwire duel and in all of the reflections on the life and history of past record-holders Ruth and Maris, there was hardly a mention of Josh Gibson. The omission is noteworthy. Gibson is considered by many as the greatest power hitter ever to hold a bat in any baseball league in the United States. He played from 1930 to 1946. In the 1931 season, at the age of nineteen, he hit seventy-five homeruns in one season, a feat that no one has even approached.

Perhaps the reason that Gibson is an unsung hero is that he played mostly in what was known as the Negro League. His record was set at a time when, because of fear and ignorance, blacks and whites could not play in the same league. And, for any who might think this other league was inferior, we should realize that Negro League teams played against the white teams hundreds of times and compiled a three-to-one winning average against them.

According to some accounts, Gibson hit 962 homeruns in his seventeen-year career and compiled a lifetime batting average of .391. In 1972, he was inducted posthumously into the National Baseball Hall of Fame.

I wouldn't have known of Josh Gibson except for a recent e-mail sent by an African-American to several friends. He started the note by saying: "Please share with your children, grandchildren, and brothers and sisters everywhere: the homerun record has not been broken!"

He went on to detail Gibson's stellar career and to extol his athletic virtues. He wanted to set the record straight and to let the world know who the homerun hero really is.

I then found my mind racing to the unsung hero of our hearts, Jesus Christ. Lost in the clutter of a world consumed with lesser things, our Lord and His unsurpassed accomplishments not only go unnoticed but also are often unwelcome to many who do not want to know—lest they become morally accountable to someone beside themselves.

This fear and ignorance is not unlike the resistance that forced Christ to live and work outside the arenas where others strutted their stuff to advance their own causes and serve their own agendas. I'm reminded of one of the songs that echo through the Christmas season, "Sweet little Jesus boy . . . We didn't know who you was."

As followers of Christ, it is our privilege to become advocates of the most accomplished person who has ever lived. Like my friend, who felt compelled to remind his world of Josh Gibson, we ought to be ready and willing publicists for the King of Kings.

The spectacularly gracious works of our Savior and friend were never intended to be treasures that we hoard for our own enjoyment. His goodness is meant to be a testimony to a watching world of the reality of His power and personal care for all those who trust Him.

The psalmist wrote: "May God be gracious to us and bless us and make his face to shine upon us, that your way may be known on earth, your saving power among all nations . . . God, our God, shall bless us . . . let all the ends of the earth fear him!" (Psalm 67:1–2, 6–7).

Opportunities to communicate the reality of God's greatness abound. When others recognize some obvious blessing in our lives, it is a prime moment to turn the spotlight on Him. We should make known answers to prayer, giving God the full credit.

The most powerful statement of all is the witness of a transformed life. When they ask why we are different, then their hearts are ready to hear of our God.

TOO GOOD TO MISS

Gary Foster was a homeless, down-on-your-luck kind of guy wandering the streets of Chicago when he happened across a signed, undesignated check for five thousand dollars. Needless to say, the temptation to find a way to cash it and upgrade his lifestyle was overwhelming. He thought of his wife and children, who could have a Christmas worth getting up for. He could go home and provide for them in the way he had always hoped he could.

The temptation was so overwhelming that he kept the check in his pocket for the whole next day, wrestling about what he should do. He may have lost his home, but he clearly had not lost his values. As he said, "It just wouldn't be the honest thing to do to cash the check."

So he went to a homeless shelter, where a financial adviser helped him with plans to return the check. When he called the construction company that had issued the check and told them he would be glad to bring the check by, they told him rather coldly not to come, but to put it in the mail. No "Thank you." No word of appreciation for his honesty. Evidently no thought of even a small reward for a good deed that would save the company a lot of grief as well as some of their own money.

This story hit the news in Chicago just before Christmas. As you can imagine, there was an outpouring of sympathy for the finder of the check, and many people were miffed at the construction company for what appeared to be a Scrooge-like reaction. If it weren't for the quick response of Pastor James Meeks and the Salem Baptist Church on Chicago's South Side, it would have been little more than another emotion-stirring story.

After hearing the tale, Pastor Meeks went to great lengths to locate the homeless man and invited him to their morning worship service the following Sunday. During the service, Gary Foster was given the opportunity to tell the story of his unusually noble response. Pastor Meeks then handed him a one-thousand-dollar check and told him that some of the businessmen in his church would guarantee him a job. Because, as the pastor said, "Someone in Chicago has to stand up and make the statement that in our town, honesty pays."

What is especially significant is that all the major media in Chicago showed up to cover the "rest of the story." That Sunday night and Monday morning, the newscasts and papers were full of what happened at Salem Baptist.

It reminds me of Christ's words in Matthew 5 when He told us that we were to be the light of the world, that a city on a hill could not be hidden, and that if you have the light you don't hide it under a barrel. Christ went on to urge us to live out our good works in such a way that a watching world could not help but notice and glorify our Father who is in heaven.

On that Sunday, Chicago was made very much aware that God's people valued honesty and that the church would take its place in the community to honor what was right and good. I'm thankful that, on this occasion, it was the church that made the statement. That's just how it should be. But to our shame, the church is often the last place that virtue is publicly displayed in ways so dramatic that the world can't help but notice.

My friend James Meeks leads us to a higher standard for the work of Christ in the world. We can preach about honesty in the face of a world that has traded in this now-rare commodity in favor of expediency and greed. We can express anger about sin and call the world toward what is right in the most passionate and eloquent ways. Yet if we don't flesh out our proclamations with actions that illustrate our commitment, our sermons become little more than the rattle of our theological skeletons.

Few outside the church really care about what we say behind closed doors on Sundays. But let our light hit the streets in meaningful, compelling ways, and a hungry world will notice. If we are to be about the business of being light in the darkness, we need to remember that Christ taught us that it is our noticeably good works, not just our good words, that bring praise and honor to Him.

WHAT DO THEY SEE?

Gandhi was asked by a friend, "If you are so intrigued with Jesus Christ, why don't you become a Christian?" Reportedly Gandhi replied, "When I meet a Christian who is a follower of Christ, I might consider it."

Gandhi's statement reminds me of what motivates a friend of mine who works on college campuses with international students. He relates that Mao Tse-tung came to America eager for a Western education and for exposure to Christianity. After observing the Christians around him, however, Mao's curiosity turned to disillusionment, and his heart and mind then shifted to Marxism. We all know the rest of the story.

Is it possible that somehow in our pilgrimage we have created a Christianity that bears little resemblance to the reality of the person of Christ?

Unfortunately, the face of Christianity often poses a distorted view of the authentic Christ. Thus, the watching world frequently sees something less than Christ. People may see a stoic or stodgy visage. They may sense our unsettledness and even anger at being marginalized and maligned by the culture at large. Or they may see a blurred image of Christ, because the way that we represent Him in our lives is hardly different from the way they live. We, like them, are consumed by greed, power, and position. We love our friends and hate our enemies. We pursue comfort and resist sacrifice. We are more interested in advancing our careers than in using our careers to advance the cause of Christ.

Any graffiti artist knows how to take a valuable piece of art and quickly distort it. The stroke of a pen superimposes a pair of glasses, a turned-down corner at the mouth, or a goatee. Is it possible that we have added graffiti to our Lord's face? Perhaps we've forgotten that He must be the singular pursuit and radiant reflection of our lives.

Christ started His ministry by calling disciples to "follow me" (Matthew 4:19). Followership is the primal call of Christianity. To come after Christ means to make Him the passionate pursuit of our existence.

Our lives are like the solar system. The sun at the center gives light and warmth and defines the direction and destination of everything else. In the same way, Christ should be our center. The light of His life, love, and character should be reflected by our lives. We must let Him determine exactly who we are and what we are doing.

Unfortunately, while happy to call ourselves Christians, rarely do we place Christ at the center of our lives. Instead, it's career, accumulation of wealth, friends, retirement, self, or some other commodity. Christ ends up as simply one of many things that we pursue.

For those early disciples who heard the primal call of Christ to "follow me," the issue was clear: What would be the central focus of their lives? Would it be the nets that they held as career fishermen? Nets that symbolized everything that they were accustomed to—their security, potential prosperity, stability? The things they got up for in the morning, that gave them worth and value and a sense of identity? Or would they be willing to drop their nets and follow Him?

And so it must be with us. Our nets are those things in our lives that occupy the center. Whether plans, friends, wealth, security, comfort, power, or position, there is nothing of greater value than the preeminent person of Christ. It's a matter of values. Would we say to Him, as we look at our nets and then into His face, that we value those nets more than we value Him?

When Christ is the singular pursuit of our lives, He alone becomes our defining influence. The closer we get, the more His love, justice, mercy, grace, and righteousness radiate from our lives.

I keep wondering . . . if Gandhi had met me, would he have seen Christ? Would he have seen, through my attitudes, actions, and responses to others, the Christ with whom he was so intrigued?

BARRICADING THE CROSS

I n case you hadn't noticed, it's election year again, with all the bumper stickers, sound bites, mudslinging, and speechmaking. I must confess I'm looking forward to the prospect. I am fascinated by the election process and charged by the issues. In reflective moments I sometimes wonder if I might have ended up in politics if God hadn't had other plans for me.

Which makes what I'm about to say seem contradictory.

One of the most damaging things that Christians have done in our generation is to politicize the gospel. And I fear we could magnify the problem in this political year.

Before you take offense, let me affirm the importance for all of us to be good citizens and to exercise our individual right to hold our government accountable for righteousness. All of us should support candidates who will promote the values that truly benefit society—the values that reflect God's character and truth.

But . . .

When our political action confuses political agendas with Christ, we compromise His uniqueness and independence. We become guilty of building barricades to the Cross. Many who need Christ can't see Him because they sense He comes with a political agenda. To some, becoming a Christian means they might have to sign the Contract with America. In addition, our behavior and attitudes in the political process have sometimes made us less than winsome representatives of Christ.

Even terminology can cause problems. For instance, I find myself asking why a political group is called the *Christian* Coalition. Much of what it espouses has little to do with lifting the name of Christ, and even less with calling the lost to Him—which is at the heart of the Christian enterprise. You don't have to be a Christian to join the Coalition, and many fine Christians feel uncomfortable with the Coalition's political perspectives. I applaud many of the Coalition's efforts, particularly in the moral arena. I just wish it had taken a different name.

We cause significant damage when we confuse people about the nature of Christ as the lover of their souls and the nature of Christianity as available for all. Republicans, Democrats, liberals, conservatives—all need a clear view of this compelling Christ, unclouded from the mists of politics.

As my friend Tony Evans says, "When Christ returns, He won't be riding a donkey or an elephant." It's a sobering thought that the only view of Christ many will ever see is the view they see in us. The most important thing in an election year is being sure that we build no unnecessary barriers to the gospel. There is only one legitimate offense, and that is the offense of the Cross.

One of the most challenging times in my pastoral ministry was when politics became particularly intense and some parishioners began to ratchet up the pressure to get political on the literature table and in the pulpit. I often shared their political passion. But there was a higher agenda that found deeper passion in my heart. It was the passion to preserve our church as a place where people of any political stripe could come and without hindrance hear the eternally strategic message of a Christ who transcends earthside interests and calls all people to Himself.

This is not to say that we don't care about legitimate issues of biblical morality. We must compassionately proclaim truth in clear and compelling ways. What we cannot do is politicize our proclamation or damage the truth with less than Christlike attitudes. We must persuade all persons, regardless of where they fall on the political spectrum, that first and foremost we care about them as individuals, seeking to minister to them with the love of Christ.

Polycarp, early martyr of the church, refused to recant his faith in Christ. When the soldiers arrived to take him to the stake, he invited them into his home and ordered his servants to feed them and meet their every need. That attitude is equally important in the political process. May those who oppose the values we hold find our hearts so compassionate and genuine that they are drawn to the Christ who has made the compelling difference in our lives.

STORY TIME

Of all my academic experiences, kindergarten was my favorite. I enjoyed the new independence, recess, and the naps. But I particularly looked forward to story time.

It has now become story time in the body of Christ. Unless we have compelling stories to tell, we will become increasingly ineffective for Christ.

As followers of Christ, we face a tension. He has commissioned us to go into all the world and preach the gospel (Mark 16:15), yet the world operates in direct opposition to the gospel.

In former generations, when society claimed a biblical moral base, this tension was not so severe. But the modern mentality is increasingly foreign to a biblical mindset. Relativism and pluralism have erased any authoritative pronouncements of right and wrong. The leading-edge theories of deconstructionism and revisionism have eroded objectivity in thinking.

As society has moved from its moral reference point, new agendas have gained political momentum: abortion, homosexual rights, self-fulfillment at any cost. Such issues now place Christians as threats to "progress." Our views are mocked in TV sitcoms, ignored in public discourse.

The new rush to pursue pleasure at any cost has also brought tremendous problems to our nation. The increasing levels of pain and despair, both personally and socially, distract hearts from the proclamation of truth.

What, then, are believers to do? Stand with our Bibles tucked under our arms, watching helplessly as society rushes toward self-destruction?

The strategy of Scripture focuses on stories. Jesus said we could best persuade people by the compelling outcomes of righteousness in our lives. "Let your light shine before others, so that they may see your good works and give glory to your Father who is in heaven" (Matthew 5:16). Peter underscored the same strategy (1 Peter 2:12).

Though our world may discount, slander, and oppose us, it cannot help but notice the irrefutable results of righteousness in our lives.

The New Testament church ministered in a world even more hostile than ours. Yet the early believers produced such compelling results in their lives that after just a few generations, the Roman Empire affirmed the very system of truth it had sought to stamp out.

Productive families who live according to the righteous standards of God's Word make a strong statement for Christ. As families around us degenerate, people will want to know what makes us different.

Our lives can tell stories of relative good health in a society plagued by self-induced diseases. Of faithful financial stewardship in a day of economic uncertainty. Of love that reaches across ethnic and cultural lines in a world increasingly divided by diversity.

Jesus meant stories like the African-American church that sought to buy property in a neighborhood noted for racism. When the church encountered resistance, it did not retaliate. Instead, knowing that the neighborhood was suffering high unemployment and poverty, it opened an office where lawyers, physicians, and other professionals from the church offered practical help. Those actions melted the extremism and opened hearts to the gospel.

Or consider the Dallas church that asked a judge to give it responsibility for one juvenile offender. The church offered to mentor the young man for six months. The venture was so successful that the judge now regularly calls the pastor for help with other offenders.

Such churches do not have to scream at evil to be effective. Without compromising truth, they reach out to their communities with compassion, drawing hurting people to Christ.

Compelling stories of righteousness build a platform for the liberating truths of the gospel. When our lives reflect the undeniably positive results of obedience, the world is more likely to listen.

When Christ spoke of our posture toward the world, He said that He did not want to remove us from the world (John 17:15) but to use us in the world (vv. 16–19). And, as the text notes, our usability is directly linked to our relationship to and application of God's Word in our lives.

The verifiable, compelling stories of the results of righteousness in our lives provide irrefutable evidence of the truths we embrace and catch the attention of those who would otherwise write us off.

In fact, it's not only story time, but show-and-tell as well. As the saying goes, "It's better to light one candle than to curse the darkness."

COMPASSION AND THE CRUCIBLE

Few things have been more unsettling to the Christian community than the gay and lesbian movement coming out of the closet. Behavior that most Americans would have considered shameful a few short decades ago is now openly promoted in our streets, our classrooms, and our courts. To our dismay, the cause is empowered by political forces from state capitals to Washington, D.C.

We who affirm what Scripture says about homosexual behavior must now form a biblical response to those who promote this lifestyle. Obviously, responding in ridicule is inconsistent with the way God distinguishes between the sin and the sinner. His redemptive love welcomes all to the liberating power of Jesus Christ.

As we seek to form our response, we find ourselves wrestling with how to keep society from celebrating homosexual behavior as a legitimate alternative. We work to stem the tide politically, with legislation and ballot initiatives. We tackle the challenge on the educational front, at meetings of the school board.

But one thing rarely heard in our strategy sessions is that homosexuals, like all of us, need to know Jesus Christ. If we believe in the authority of Scripture as God's revealed truth, then homosexuality is a matter that not only has earth-side ramifications but eternal ramifications as well.

Our dilemma deepens as we read reports suggesting that homosexuality is genetically dictated. For years, experts traced homosexuality to early childhood influences or personal choice. Some homosexuals are using the recent reports to conclude that "God made us this way," so it's okay to express that sexual preference.

Even if further research could prove genetic factors in homosexuality, it's clear that God didn't make us this way. When He created the human race, He started with a man and a woman, designing them to complement each other spiritually and emotionally and physically.

According to Genesis 3, sin entered the scene by Adam's choice and totally rearranged what God had created. That cataclysmic moment ushered in the damaging, deadening effects of sin, to our bodies as well as our souls. Homosexuality, both in terms of propensity and practices, is a direct outgrowth of the universal problem of sin.

Understanding this should give us a clearer perspective on the issue. It doesn't really make much difference if homosexuality is genetic or environmental. It is one among many of the problems of our fallen race.

Before God, we are all sinners. We all struggle with the propensity and practice of sin, though in different areas. We may be culturally conditioned to assume that some sins are more repugnant than others, but all sins are a deep offense to God.

The good news is that when mankind fell into the ravages of sin, God Himself entered that fallen place. Instead of annihilating the sinners, He reached out to them with the promise of redemption. That promise was fulfilled when Christ died on the cross for all of our sins.

Those who believe are made alive in Christ. We have His guarantee that the curse of sin will be ultimately removed in eternity. Until then, we receive supernatural advantages for our struggle against sin: the convicting and guiding power of the Word of God, the enabling of the Spirit of God, and the support and encouragement of the people of God.

Having given us all these benefits, Christ sends us out to reach others—any kind of others—who are also victims of sin. In courage and compassion, we announce His standards of righteousness and offer His gracious liberation from sin.

Even a casual analysis of the church's response to the homosexual issue finds that many of us are long on anger and short on mercy. We need to remind each other that, regardless of the social aims of homosexual activists, no one is exempt from the need of a Savior. Above and beyond every temporal concern, eternal issues must drive our hearts and minds to the compassion of Christ, the One who came to seek and to save that which was lost.

Thankfully, there are many churches and Christian organizations across the country that effectively reach out to homosexuals. We must pray for these ministries, support them, and somehow train our hearts to a compassionate response—not just to some sinners, but to all.

After all, isn't biblical compassion really a matter of one beggar telling another where to find bread?

NO WASTED SORROW

Only a few weeks ago, I stood on a small strip of sand along one of the hundreds of bends in the Curaray River, deep in the Ecuadorian jungle. It is a profound place, not simply because of the jungle's beauty and mystery, but because thirty-seven years ago, five gifted young men gave their lives for the cause of Christ.

The five men—Jim Elliot, Ed McCully, Peter Fleming, Roger Youderian, and Nate Saint—had affectionately named the spot "Palm Beach." They had flown there and set up camp with the purpose of reaching the killer tribe known as the Aucas. They had built a brief but hopeful relationship with three of the Indians who visited them on the beach. Then suddenly, a killing party rushed out from the jungle, hurling spears and leaving all five dead.

My wife and I stood on the beach as the river rolled by, thinking of the young men's bodies thrown into the river, snagged on debris for five days until a search party arrived to bury them several yards behind where we stood.

In 1956, it seemed a tragic waste of manpower. But God has marvelous ways of taking our worst tragedies and turning them into His most glorious triumphs. Word soon reached the states, as *Life* magazine and major news services gave the killings in-depth coverage. And all across this continent, hundreds, perhaps thousands, of young people on college campuses stood to say, "I'll take their place." The new wave of missionaries took the torch of Christ from those five men and carried it around the globe.

An old Indian sat in the back of the dugout canoe that guided us down the river to Palm Beach. I learned that he had been a member of the killing party. But on the beach we stood together as brothers in Christ.

The head of the killing party, the one who speared pilot Nate Saint, had also become a Christian. When someone asked him what he would do when he got to heaven, he said, "I will look for Nate Saint, throw my arms around him, and thank him for bringing the gospel to our jungle." Then he added, "And Nate Saint will throw his arms around me and welcome me home, for we are friends in Jesus Christ."

God never wastes our sorrows or dead-ends the sacrifices of His servants.

I don't think my life will ever be quite the same after standing in that place. I saw that Christ gives us a cause not only worth living for, but also worth dying for when necessary. As a colleague of mine thoughtfully remarked, our world encourages us to spend much time discovering our identity and looking for meaning in life. Those five men stood in bold contrast to our cultural perspective.

Those five did not allow their zeal and vision to be eclipsed by fruitless searches for identity and meaning. They were not on introspective searches; they were on a mission for the greatest cause that this world knows. They were not into discovery; they were into doing. In the daily routine of obedience, they faithfully lived out what God had called them to do. The meaning in their lives came through getting busy in what God wanted them to do.

As I thought about this Christmas season, I recalled that *doing* was the model of Jesus Christ as well. Though He had the grandest, most glorious identity in the universe, He let go of all the benefits and privileges, all the perks for paradise, to obediently get busy about the task of redemption. To serve the needs of our fallen race, He humbly endured the agonies of this fallen place.

Because Jesus Christ was a willing and obedient doer, God has exalted Him to the highest place. He has given Him the name that is above every name. Therefore, "at the name of Jesus every knee should bow . . . and every tongue confess that Jesus Christ is Lord" (Philippians 2:9–11). Christmas teaches us that we are called, not to a pilgrimage of self-discovery but to a supernaturally empowered life of surrendered doing.

Those five men at the beach were willing to push their lives to the brink because they served the one who had pushed His life to the brink for them.

Like those five, Jesus tasted death. But hell's party was canceled after only three days. Like trick candles on a birthday cake, the flame He ignited could never be put out. Today, those of us who know the Christ of Christmas still walk in His inextinguishable light.

Christmas is about surrendered doing on behalf of the one who loved us and gave Himself for us. On behalf of the one who never dead-ends His heroes.

THE TRUE ALTERNATIVE LIFESTYLE

Having learned many years ago that New Year's resolutions are tough to manage for 365 days, let me begin 1993 with a prediction instead. I predict that those who live authentically Christian lives will increasingly find themselves part of a distinct subculture, one that runs against the grain of America's current sociopolitical momentum.

In this new era, Christians will likely be seen as obstacles to social progress. We may even face new ridicule and intolerance—all because we hold to Judeo-Christian absolutes, not only as our personal standards but also for the safety and well-being of society.

Granted, I'm not a prophet and do not claim the stature of divine prediction. Yet even a casual analysis of the current climate in America indicates that this scenario is at least a high probability.

Given that, a strategic question looms before us: What are Christians to do in this increasingly hostile environment? How are we to witness in a world that no longer wants to hear what we have to say? As Francis Schaeffer put it, "How shall we then live?"

First of all, we must resist the temptation to despair, and guard against angry, hostile responses to our world's hatred. God's Word clearly calls us to a redemptive compassion for all kinds of people, even the worst elements of society (Luke 15).

In its early days, Christianity flourished with such great power that it caught the world's attention—even though believers lived in an environment of tremendous resistance morally, politically, and spiritually. Their secret? They followed the strategy Jesus gave in passages like Matthew 5:14, 16. "You are the light of the world . . .

Let your light shine before others, so that they may see your good works and give glory to your Father who is in heaven."

The power of their witness rested not in words their world would hear but in deeds their world would see. Likewise, in our day, we can be sure that when the world stops listening to us, it will still be looking.

The apostle Peter also spoke to a counterculture Christianity that was suffering repercussions from its commitment to Christ. "Keep your conduct among the Gentiles honorable, so that when they speak against you as evildoers, they may see your good deeds and glorify God on the day of visitation (1 Peter 2:12).

Peter's principle is this: If we maintain righteousness within our lives, families, and churches, ultimately the contrast with the world's unrighteousness will become clear.

As people around us feel the consequences of unrighteousness—in terms of disease, disorientation, and dysfunctional lives—they cannot help but notice the relative health and wholeness of our lives. At that moment, they will be ready to listen when we say that Jesus Christ is "the way, the truth, and the life."

This strategy, of course, is not as quick or as compelling as the cries for political activism. But the power of Christianity in the days ahead will increasingly depend on whether God's people are courageously and compassionately committed to the exercise of authentic righteousness.

An unwavering, non-negotiable commitment to righteousness in every area of our lives must be our foremost priority.

Those of us who are parents have an added responsibility. We must also guard our children against the subtle subterfuge of a secularized environment, teaching them, both by our example and our word, the importance and the power of authentic Christianity.

This commitment to righteousness in our personal lives and families will then affect our churches and ultimately our community as a whole.

Scripture has much to say about righteousness in terms of our family, our money, our behavior in the marketplace, our morality, our attitudes, the way we spend our time, and the things we think about. And the Bible promises great rewards for those who practice righteousness. While never fully exempt from our society's problems, we will develop internal qualities that will shine ever brighter in a culture that is growing increasingly dark.

During the last several years, there's been much discussion about "alternative lifestyles." Various groups choose not to follow society's normal pattern of behavior. More and more in the days ahead, Christianity will become the true alternative lifestyle. If lived courageously, compassionately, and correctly, it will be the power of God, through us, unto the salvation of those who see.

WITH LOVE TO 11J

My seat assignment for the Saturday evening flight was 11H. When I entered the huge coach section of the DC-10, I saw a young woman sitting next to a window on the far side of the plane. She was obviously distraught, her face buried in her hands.

As I approached my seat, I realized we would be travel partners on that hour-and-a-half jaunt into Toronto. *If the plane isn't too crowded, maybe I can get another seat,* I thought. I was headed for a week of ministry two hours north of the city, and my portfolio was full of work.

Predictably, the Spirit of God began to transform my self-focused response. What would Christ have done if He had walked onto this plane? His life was committed to loving others, especially those in need. I knew He would have wanted to sit next to her, that His heart would have been touched by the burden of her heart, and that He would have reached out to help—even if it meant sacrificing His plans.

As I sat down, the young woman lifted her face, tears running down her cheeks. "I miss my daddy!" I immediately recognized she was mentally handicapped.

I tried to start a conversation with her, but her one-word answers didn't go far. Between sobs, she told me she was afraid to fly in the dark. I pulled down all the shades I could reach. A few minutes later, I changed her watch to Toronto time. I wondered what people around me might be thinking. The man behind me found her to be such a distraction that he asked the flight attendant if he could change seats.

Christa talked nonstop most of the flight—to me, to her friend that she had left at home, and whenever possible, to the flight attendant. After the attendant brought peanuts and pop, she kept asking, "Why can't we have something else? I'm hungry." Given the price of the tickets, I thought she had a good point.

Halfway to Toronto, the flight attendant asked me if I would like a free drink. Needless to say, I declined.

"Where are you from, Christa?" I asked.

"Wisconsin."

"What part of Wisconsin?"

"Union Grove."

I could hardly believe it. One of the outstanding Christian homes for the handicapped is located in Union Grove. "Christa, are you from Shepherds?"

"Yes," she said, "and I'm going to Toronto where my daddy lives, and tomorrow he will take me to Peoples Church."

I was suddenly struck with the meaning of the moment. It was as if God had directly assigned me to help this precious lamb from a Christian home, so innocent and so vulnerable, to get from Chicago to Toronto. Of the more than three hundred seats on this plane, He had put me next to her.

At the baggage claim, I ended up next to the man who had asked for a seat change. "Do you know that lady?" he asked.

"No."

"Are you a therapist?"

"No."

"A psychologist?"

"No."

"Then what do you do?"

"I'm a minister."

He paused, then said reflectively, "I knew you had to have something extra, to do what you did on that plane." Then his luggage came, and he was gone.

Could this be what our Lord was talking about when He said we are the light of the world? When people see our good works, they notice a difference and glorify our Father in heaven (Matthew 5:16). I pray that others will cast the light across that man's path and that he will come to know the One who alone gives us the strength to love.

The next morning, as I ministered in northern Ontario, I related this experience. After the service, two couples came up. "We're from Peoples Church," they said, "and we know Christa. Her dad will be delighted to know that you helped her on the trip."

I got the greatest letter from Christa's dad.

Quite frankly, my ministry to her was rather unrewarding. She did not have the capacity to understand or appreciate much of what I did. In fact, if I were to see Christa today, I doubt she would even remember me.

But I learned a good lesson on that trip. When God calls us to love, He may have in mind a far different agenda from what we envision. Answers for someone who is watching. Comfort for a concerned dad. And joy in my own heart to be a messenger of God's love.

When people don't respond to our love, if they reject our love, even if they misuse and abuse our love . . . it's okay. God calls us to love and to let Him manage the results.

THE HIGHEST HONOR

My dad stood there, hat and coat in hand. As I continued to play with my newly opened Christmas toys, I heard him say, "Joe, why don't you come with me?"

That question, asked nearly every Christmas, put me in tension. For me, Christmas was a celebration that included gifts to be assembled, showed off, and enjoyed. Add Mom's cooking and some family and friends, and Christmas was complete.

My dad knew better. For him, Christmas was more than a celebration of Christ's birth.

The highest form of honor is not celebration; it is imitation. Celebration, even at Christmas, can have a selfish bent. Many celebrate primarily for the gain of a day off, a party, or a good time. It would be a far greater compliment to imitate the truth, values, and behavior of the one whose life we celebrate.

In my last year of seminary, I could tell the theology majors because they talked, gestured, and phrased their conversations like their theology professors. It was the same with the Christian education majors and the pastoral majors. We honored the faculty and gave proof of their influence upon us by the way our lives and minds reflected theirs.

The fact that my father was leaving that Christmas afternoon was proof that his maturity in Christ had taken him beyond celebration.

For Jesus Christ, Christmas was not warm, convenient, or comfortable. We must keep reminding ourselves in this Santa-ized, materialized blur called Christmas that on the first Christmas, Christ stepped out to begin the central act of God's redemptive plan. And it cost Him to do it.

It's not that gifts are inappropriate at Christmas; Jesus Christ gave a gift. The significance of Christmas lies in the fact that Christ gave Himself—a gift that cost Him dearly.

Think for a moment of what it meant for an all-present God to be incarcerated in a body of human flesh—a baby's body at that. Or what it meant for Him to relinquish His rights and privileges as God to be made "a little lower than the angels" and to arrive in "the form of a servant."

Jesus paid the cost of His gift in the currency of His divine glory and acclaim, trading them for the jeers and taunts of a fickle crowd. "Criminal," they called Him, instead of "Christ." His gift would culminate on a bloodstained cross where His sinless body bore the weight of our sins.

Jesus Christ presented to our world a redemptive gift that cost Him much. That's why my dad was on his way out the front door. In a large old house two blocks west of ours, lived an elderly widow who loved the Lord but had no children and no family. She spent every holiday alone in that house. And every Christmas my dad, in the midst of celebration, gave the gift of himself.

He would grab his coat and walk down the street to knock on the door of a lonely lady. Her house sat on a big lot. She had a wealthy estate. What she didn't have was something that money couldn't buy: a gift of love and companionship.

What do you give to someone who has everything but that? Like Christ, you pay a price. You give yourself.

Around all of our lives there are people who do not need much of this world's goods but who long for a touch from heaven through our lives.

Who are the people you could phone on Christmas day? Who didn't send you a card last year but should get a card from you with an encouraging note? Whom are you having over? Are there some who will go nowhere if they don't hear from you? Are there some who cannot repay?

While there is a sense of redemption in touching those who need the gift of your love, there are many others as well who need the saving gift of Jesus Christ. This is the season to let them know what Christmas really means.

A well-chosen card that clearly communicates that Jesus is the reason for the season is a good beginning. Then consider offering an invitation to dinner or to a Christmas concert or pageant where the gospel is made plain. There could be no greater joy than to see the gospel come alive in hearts through the sacrificial gift of Christ.

Indelibly etched in my memory are those two or three times when I stood up from my toys, grabbed my coat, put my hand in Dad's, and walked down the street to spend an hour imitating Christ's gift of Himself.

This year, let's do more than celebrate Christ. Let's honor Him by imitating the selfless and costly gift of Himself.

CANDY COUNTERS AND
SOUP KITCHENS

We were on our annual Christmas trek to Chicago. Each year we brought our family to spend time with Grandpa and Grandma and visit the museums. This year we decided to finish our Christmas shopping at suburban Woodfield Mall. In the midst of the all the fun and excitement, one of us noticed that little three-and-a-half-year-old Matthew was gone.

Terror immediately struck our hearts. We had heard the horror stories: little children kidnapped in malls, rushed to a restroom, donned in different clothes and altered hairstyle, and then swiftly smuggled out, never to be seen again. To think that we could recover our son who was lost in the maze of shops and department stores in this multi-tiered marketplace was almost beyond our hope.

We split up, each taking an assigned location. Mine was the parking lot. I'll never forget that night—kicking through the newly fallen snow, calling out his name at the top of my lungs. I felt like an abject fool, yet my concern for his safety outweighed all other feelings.

Unsuccessful, I trudged back to our meeting point. My wife, Martie, had not found him, nor had my mother. And then my dad appeared, holding little Matthew by the hand. Our hearts leapt for joy.

Interestingly enough, Matthew was not traumatized. He hadn't been crying. To him, there had been no problem

I asked my father where he had found him.

"The candy counter," he replied. "You should have seen him. His eyes came just about as high as the candy. He held his little hands behind his back and moved his head back and forth, survey-ing all the luscious options."

Matthew didn't look lost. He didn't know he was lost. He was oblivious to the phenomenal danger he was in.

This is a candy-counter culture, where people who don't look lost and don't know they're lost live for consumption. At no time in the calendar does this candy-counter syndrome become more evident than during Christmas.

In this season, we have the privilege of bringing lost people to the one Person who satisfies their real internal and eternal need and who delivers them from the ultimate danger of hell.

It would be easy, however, to go through this Advent season just tipping the hat of our hearts to the newborn Savior and not realizing that the very reason for Christmas is found in the malls and in our neighborhoods.

People!

The throbbing issue this Christmas: Who cares? Who cares for their neighbors, their associates, their families? Who cares about the homeless, those locked into the downward spiral of despair in the inner city?

Many of us have found our sensitivities insulted and our con-victions offended as court rulings removed the crèches from the lawns of our city halls. It's far easier to object to that swipe of secularism than to realize that for years many of us have been liv-ing through the Christmas season with, figuratively, no crèche on the front lawns of our lives. Caught up in the swirl and storm of the holiday, who of us has taken the time to proclaim Jesus as the reason for the season?

When the Bible speaks to us about "redeeming the time, because the days are evil" (Ephesians 5:16 KJV), it affirms the necessity to creatively capture our moments for Christ.

This Christmas season offers plenty of opportunities: signifi-cant cards that tell the true Christmas story and are bathed with prayer, family letters that describe the wonderful work of Christ in your life through the past year, appropriate gifts that express a heart of concern and love. You can participate in musical outreaches of your local church—if not in the choir, then as an usher or helper, certainly by bringing a friend who needs to know Jesus Christ. This special season deserves an extra boldness to speak for Christ. When we look for opportunities, it's amazing how many we find.

Perhaps you could try something radical. Go to a mission on Christmas day, dressed in jeans and a sweatshirt, and ladle out meals to the hungry and homeless who come off the street.

Jesus Christ said, "I came to seek and to save what was lost." If that expresses the real meaning of Christmas—and it does—then shouldn't we be searching the candy counters and the soup kitchens for them, too?

I think so!

PART FOUR

TAKE UP THE SHIELD OF FAITH

One Sunday this summer, I slipped into the back row of a little village church way out in the country. The warmth and sincerity of those gathered struck me, but I was not prepared for what would happen next.

The pastor invited a woman in the congregation to come up and offer prayers for the church. She appeared well prepared as she shuffled three pages into place on the pulpit and then bowed her head, leading us in prayer.

Not long into the prayer she said, "And Lord, please be with Peter and Mary . . ." Her voice broke as she tried, haltingly, to continue. We've all felt the awkwardness when someone starts crying while offering prayer or testimony. Slowly she regained a measure of composure and continued, "We do not know, Lord, why You have seen fit to take three of our babies home in the past three years."

I was struck immediately with the weight of grief that such a small church had been asked to bear. But what she prayed next caught my heart.

She continued, still not completely in control, "Lord, we know that it is not ours to ask why, but simply to trust you. So Lord, we pray that You will teach us to trust."

Her prayer reflects a powerful sense of innocence. Not naiveté, but an innocence that is profound in its childlike faith. Her heart cry was of one who has learned the lesson God worked so hard to teach Job and his deluded friends.

Granted, asking why is not wrong. In fact, God's Word provides many solid answers to the whys that haunt our hearts in times of trouble.

For instance, God tells us He uses trials to catch our attention. As C. S. Lewis said, "God whispers to us in our pleasures and shouts to us in our pain." He catches our attention to reprove and rearrange our wandering hearts.

God uses the fallout of living in a fallen place among a fallen race to work all things together for good (Romans 8:28). He uses difficulties to strengthen our faith, develop character (James 1:1–5), and demonstrate to a watching world that our God is worthy to be worshiped and adored—even when life hammers us with devastating blows (Job 1–42).

Scripture makes it clear that while none of us is exempt from trouble, the follower of Christ has the unique edge of knowing that in the end God will bring glory from our pain.

Yet except for giving us these principles to which we can cling, God rarely answers the details of the "why" question.

We are left with the unanswered questions of "Why me?" "Why now?" "Why can't life be normal for me like it is for everyone else?" "Why do people worse than I seem to live so painlessly?"—and a dozen other "whys" whose answers elude us.

These unanswered questions can leave us somewhere between doubt and faith. They tempt us to doubt His goodness and threaten to erode our foothold in the promises and principles of His Word.

In the face of unresolved whys we are left simply to trust Him. Nevertheless, this is not a blind trust. It is a trust not in the answers and outcomes, but in the One who manages the answers and outcomes. It is a trust that hangs on to His character and refuses to let go, a trust that believes that God is a God of love.

His love for us guarantees we can trust Him and never be disappointed, that He is a good God, and, as such, He will never waste our sorrows.

His unsurpassed power gives us the confidence that no problem is too tough for Him. No difficulty is too complex. Christ's sacrifice at the cross proves there is no sin or effect of sin that He has not already covered. His resurrection guarantees us that victory is already won, and we have the promise of heaven, where all tears will be wiped away forever.

This trust is what made the woman's prayer so profound and her point so on-target. Who could explain why three children would die in that little flock? No one. But they could trust. Trust in all that God really is. Trust in all that He has promised to do.

GOOD THOUGHTS IN BAD TIMES

There's nothing like a good, old-fashioned, "in-your-face" crisis to put our relationship with God in jeopardy. When the going gets tough, Satan can steal our affections toward God by putting his deceitful spin on our experiences. Watch out for these patterns:

- Blaming God for the evil that Satan has inspired and superimposed on our lives
- Depicting God as good to others but denying us position, pleasure, or prosperity, so we conclude God is not good to us
- Making us feel we have been good but that God has not rewarded us, leaving our righteousness an empty sacrifice
- Blinding us to the fact that God can take the very worst things in our lives and orchestrate them for good and gain
- Convincing us that God's ways for us are unduly restrictive and oppressive

When Satan gets us to misinterpret God's work in our lives, he dampens our desire for God and erodes our confidence in depending fully on Him. We are left more and more to ourselves and more vulnerable to Satan's influence.

Few moments in history more graphically display this tension between our experience with life and our view of God than the interchange between Job and his wife. While both had ample reason to see life from Satan's point of view, it was Job's wife whose heart had been turned against God by their shared tragedy.

Her counsel: "Curse God and die" (Job 2:9). His perspective: "Though he slay me, I will hope in him" (13:15). Job had an intimate connection with God that could not be severed by life's circumstances, regardless of how wrenching they were. The tougher life got, the more Job felt he needed God. As Peter Kreeft points out in his *Three Philosophies of Life,* in God, "Job has everything even though he has nothing" in contrast to the godless person who has "nothing even though he has everything."

As the psalmist confidently embraced God and testified in the midst of the calamities in his life, "Though an army encamp against me, my heart shall not fear; though war arise against me, yet I will be confident . . . For he will hide me in his shelter in the day of trouble; he will conceal me under the cover of his tent; he will lift me high upon a rock" (Psalm 27:3, 5).

We must remember that Satan is the spin-doctor of hell. He is, as Christ warns us, the father of lies (John 8:44). Spiritual intimacy and aloneness rise and fall on the issue of whom we choose to believe. Eve believed Satan and plunged her life into alienation and loss. Job believed in God and was never alone—even in the depth of the misery he experienced.

We can empower our defense against the dislodging of our affections toward God through an unwavering belief in a few basic truths:

- Satan is our enemy and seeks to destroy us by alienating us from the only resource that can sustain us (1 Peter 5:8).
- It is Satan—not God—who is wicked and who has ill intentions against us (John 8:44).
- Though God permits all that comes into our lives, Satan perpetrates evil. The devil—not God—deserves the blame for initiating ill-motivated actions against us (Job 1, 2).
- God permits in our lives only those negative events that He plans in time to turn to His glory, the advance of the kingdom, and our good (Romans 8:28).

- God's laws and principles are good. They are intended to keep us out of harm's way and direct us in ways that ultimately bless and prosper our lives (Psalm 1).
- The most powerful statement we can make to a watching world is that our God is worthy of our affection and allegiance—even through rough times and when we are not blessed as others are (1 Peter 2:12).

The discipline of seeing these truths clearly and responding in light of them keeps our hearts and minds in touch with God and enables us to resist any wedge the enemy seeks to drive between us. Regardless of circumstances, we can place our unwavering trust in God, who deserves our highest allegiance, cares intensely for us, and does all things well.

CHRIST IN THE CHAOS

We know how chaotic life can get. But it's not the chaos of the busyness and confusing scramble of life that bothers me. I have finally realized that the hope of a well-ordered life without days turned upside down and inside out is a fantasy. What I find so hard to deal with is the chaotic intrusion of devastating disappointments.

But slowly I am learning that underneath the chaos, God is there, working to accomplish good and glorious things.

In the past four months I have had the privilege of ministering in the former Soviet Union and in Hong Kong.

I was in the Ukraine and Russia as part of a ministry known as the CoMission, which had been invited by a high-ranking official in the Russian Ministry of Education to teach a curriculum on Christian life and ethics to teachers in the Russian educational system. Over the past four years, the power of the gospel has flourished in ways far beyond our expectations. Heaven will resound with the harvest that has been gleaned. Through it all, we wondered why such a high-ranking official had invited us in the first place. Just three months ago, we found out.

Paul Eshleman, who is the head of the *Jesus* film project, had been invited several years earlier to have *Jesus* shown at a film festival in Moscow. It was a phenomenal breakthrough for the gospel in a country that had been closed to Christ for so long. As a result, Paul signed a contract for the film to be shown in theaters across Russia. We could hardly believe this was happening. The contract stated that the theaters would have the exclusive right to show the film, and that to protect the theaters' investment, it would not be shown on television.

Several weeks later, the film showed up on television. A Russian entrepreneur had struck a side deal for his own personal gain. The contract was breached, Christ's name dishonored, and Paul's life severely complicated in the chaos.

Three months ago at a dinner in Moscow, the Russian official who had opened this dramatic door to the work of Christ in the public schools came to the microphone. As part of his speech, he told this story: Sitting in his living room several years ago, he saw the last ten minutes of the *Jesus* film on television. It captured his curiosity. He had never seen or heard anything quite like that. Later, while walking down the street in his hometown, he passed a theater showing the film. He went in, and, as he told those gathered at the banquet, he cried twice—once when they nailed Christ's hands to the cross and again at the end when he accepted Christ as his personal Savior.

He had never told us. He couldn't because of his high position in the government. I was struck afresh that Christ works for good in the chaos of our lives.

In Hong Kong, we were thrilled by reports of the church's explosive growth in Mainland China. In the late 1940s, all the Western missionaries had been martyred or expelled. At that time, there were about one million believers in China. Dreams for the evangelization of China had been dashed, and so many who had dedicated their lives to that land suffered greatly.

Today there are more than forty million Chinese Christians. But what is truly significant is that while Christianity was once seen as the intrusion of a foreign religion, it is now a religion that has become widely accepted in China. As such it is empowered, since many no longer view it as the deception and delusion of Western culture.

I can still remember how I thought that the tragedy in Tiananmen Square had closed the door to the gospel. I had assumed that if the students had their way, China would be open to Christ. But

God was managing the chaos of that historic day toward great and grander things. Today it is reported that thousands of students at China's universities have come to Christ. This phenomenon started soon after the Tiananmen massacre, as students whose political dreams were dashed turned their despairing hearts to Christ.

When chaos strikes, remember that it's never chaotic to Christ, who works all things together for good.

HAPPINESS NOW AND THEN

The old Three Stooges line, "Are you happy or married?" might have applied to Christians decades ago if it were rephrased, "Are you happy or saved?" Some of us remember days when we often heard sermons reminding us that Christians didn't have to be such a sad and sorry lot. "After all, we have the joy of Christ in our hearts!" A friend of mine was fond of saying, "Christians who are happy in their hearts need to telephone their faces and let them know."

All of that has changed. We have finally talked ourselves into seeking the happiness we denied ourselves in generations past. The average Christian and the guy on the street look for happiness in the same places: money, comfort, pleasure, security, and dreams of bigger and better things. And so we join the crowd, ignoring the fact that we are trampling profound priorities and valued relationships in the scramble to reach our blissful destination.

To watch how we live today, one might assume that the "pursuit of happiness" phrase from the Declaration of Independence had become an addendum to the Sermon on the Mount.

Yet, given this new enthusiasm for life, at best we may have missed the point again. Not the point of being happy, but rather how one becomes happy and when and where happiness is found.

Like the masses that have rushed the goal before us, we keep wondering why we still aren't all that happy. Why the vacuum in our souls? Why the thinness in the satisfaction we had hoped for?

American Scientific magazine, in its May 1996 issue, unmasked the myths about happiness. It noted, "People have not become happier over time as their cultures have become more affluent. Even though Americans earn twice as much as they did in 1957, [the number that] are 'very happy' has declined from 35 to 29 percent." One thing is evident from the research. Happiness has little to do with wealth, the accumulation of things, and the enhancement of our significance.

According to the study, four traits tend to characterize truly happy people. They "like themselves, . . . feel in personal control, . . . are usually optimistic, . . . [and] are extroverted." Interestingly, all of these qualities are most deeply enjoyed by those who are maturing as followers of Jesus Christ. Guiltlessness and unconditional acceptance enable believers to feel right about themselves and to live above the haunting sense of personal shame. Followers of Christ also escape the controlling influences of evil and enjoy true self-control. Amid the pervasive despair in our society, we have an assured optimism in the ultimate victory of Christ and the glory of an eternity with Him. And, Scripture urges us to be others-oriented instead of selfishly withdrawn.

The article goes on to note that "religious people" and married people have a greater tendency toward happiness. This only underscores that the sources of happiness are found not in the stuff of this world or its comforts, but in growing relationships with God and intimate friends.

Scripture does not promise that life will always be a happy experience. Suffering and hardship are inevitable companions on our pilgrimage. Full and unlimited happiness is what God has in store for us in the world to come. As one writer notes, this is the "short nasty brutish world." Even Christ recognized that He had to endure the cross in the light of the joy that was set before Him.

We should never be the sad and sorry lot that we thought we were in decades past. But we must not be happiness addicts that live for the pursuit of pleasure. While we should possess an exuberance and resilience even in the toughest of times, ultimate happiness must wait for the other side. The pursuit of the believer is defined and driven by far more important commodities: righteousness, faithfulness, servanthood, contentment, justice, and compassion (1 Timothy 6:6–11).

When our happiness here reaches ecstatic dimensions, we should thank God for His unusual grace. When the road is darker than we thought, then we steady ourselves with the distant glow of the happy land ahead.

HOLIDAY CHEER

If you like holidays, this season is a real plus. Pressed into five quick and busy weeks are Thanksgiving, Christmas, and New Year's. Each comes with its own distinctive flavor, extended days off work, family, friends, festive music, an abundance of good food, and a little football.

For those of us who know Christ, the celebrations take on a particularly profound meaning. Think of all we have to be thankful for because God sent His Son to be born, live, die, and rise so that all things could be made new. This string of holidays is like a metaphor of the significant realities in our lives.

Recently my wife, Martie, was reading through a small book on the Twenty-third Psalm that we picked up in a used bookstore in England. Its author is the prominent British pastor of the last century, F. B. Meyer. When he got to the phrase "My cup runneth over," his exposition was particularly moving.

Meyer noted that all of us have cups of a different nature, some gold, some glass, some of earthenware. But Christ fills each cup with the same sweet and satisfying mixture of His grace. The reason that our cup is so abundantly full and sweet, Meyer explained, is because the cup that our Savior drank at the cross was so full of sorrow and shame.

"Consider the ingredients of Christ's cup—the shame and spitting; the pain and anguish; the physical torture; . . . the bitterness of our sins, which were made to meet in Him; the guilt of our curse, which He voluntarily assumed; the equivalent of our punishment which was imputed to Him."

Meyer went on to say it was as if "the human race stood in one long line, each with a cup of hemlock in his hands; and Christ, passing along, took from each his cup and poured its contents into the vast beaker which He carried: so that, on the cross, He 'tasted death for every man'" [Hebrews 2:9].

"Our cup is one of joy," said Meyer, "because His cup was one of sorrow. Our cup is one of blessedness, because His was one of God-forsakenness."

Meyer continued, "Never forget the cost at which your brightest moments have been made possible."

Meyer specified the bounty in our cup that we often take for granted: Good health, friendships and love, comforts of home, the joys of the mind, and more. "Now and again there is a dash of extra sweetness poured into life's cup—some special deliverance; some unlooked-for interposition; some undeserved and unusual benediction—sent apparently for no other object than to satisfy God's passion for giving."

When Meyer got to this point, my heart was struck with the bountiful provision of our God. "But whatever blessing is in our cup, it is sure to run over. With Him, the calf is always the fatted calf; the robe is always the best robe; the joy is unspeakable; the peace passeth understanding; the grace is so abundant that the recipient has all-sufficiency for all things, and abounds in every good work. There is no grudging in God's benevolence; He does not measure out His goodness as the apothecary counts his drops and measures his drachms, slowly and exactly, drop by drop."

As Meyer notes, the greatest blessings in our cup are the mixture of spiritual joy, satisfaction, and peace in our communion with Christ. That sense of His full presence and the assurance of His power and protection in whatever life might hold for us is the greatest of all the blessings of God upon our lives.

Because our cups do run over, to whom are we giving the overflow? The blessings of our Lord are not to be hoarded, but to be generously and abundantly shared with others.

Meyer concludes by exhorting us to take our cups and drink with gratitude. "Some appear to think that God does not mean them to be thoroughly happy; and if they drink their cups of joy, it must be on the sly or with words of apology. Some drink only half; or if they drink at all, they instill some bitter ingredient of their own, lest the draught should be too delicious. How often we forget that God has given us all things richly to enjoy!" [1 Timothy 6:17].

Thanksgiving is the only appropriate response to Christ, who was born to make all things new.

Think of the psalm's ecstatic benediction, "My cup overflows. Surely goodness and mercy shall follow me all the days of my life, and I shall dwell in the house of the Lord forever" (vv. 5–6).

WHERE SHOULD WE PRAY?

Now that the Contract with America is in full swing, consideration of a prayer-in-school amendment has been pushed back to a later date. This, no doubt, concerns a lot of us who fear that the issue will be once again doomed to be deep-sixed.

Actually, I don't know that we have given a lot of thought to the significance of prayer in the public schools as it is presently envisioned.

Some of us remember when we stood in class and recited the Lord's Prayer with its emphasis on the Father, His will, heaven, kingdom, the divine provision of bread, the importance of forgiveness, and the treachery of temptation.

The prayer amendment as proposed is far removed from that substantive experience. At the most, we might get a moment of silence when students can elect to pray to whomever they wish.

Some have wondered why an official moment of silence is necessary. They point out that students can already pray silently anytime and anywhere they want in school.

Others wonder if we don't put the real meaning of prayer at risk if there are quiet prayers to Allah, Buddha, Satan, and who-knows-what-else during that moment.

At best, it seems to me, the plan may help restore to the schools a sense of a transcendent being. That in itself may be worth the fuss. But it will be symbol more than substance. Real prayer is about praise and petitions to a real God who both hears and answers.

Our greater concern should be that we as Christians rarely pray at all—anywhere.

Shouldn't we all give some thought to focusing our energies on prayer in our homes, churches, small groups, and personal times of intercession? There is less time spent in prayer on Sundays than ever before. In many homes, outside of mealtimes, there is no prayer at all. There are few small groups dedicated solely to prayer, and I find myself wondering whatever happened to a central meeting at church dedicated to prayer.

Our fervor for the prayer-in-school issue does ring a little hollow, given our general lack of concern for prayer in our own lives and gatherings. In fact, if there were more prayers where prayers should be, the issue of prayer in school might not seem so critical.

I also find myself wondering why we are so ready to embrace political causes that rally our energies against the faults of others, while often ignoring the issues of our own consecration, growth, and development. While it may be easier to raise enthusiasm for public agendas that are important to us, it is still more important to commit ourselves to agendas that honor spiritual growth and development in our own lives.

Maybe we have forgotten how centrally important prayer is to the Christian community.

If prayer were more prevalent and given a higher profile in our programming, we would foster a greater sense of the reality and centrality of the transcendent God—the One who is worthy of our prayers and praise regardless of our life situation (Psalm 148) and who genuinely cares for us and is ready to give grace to help in times of need (Hebrews 4:14–16).

More prayer at home would help us raise a generation that also believed in a worthy, caring God.

It would expand our children's view of life beyond the confines of Nintendo. The windows of their hearts would be open to an awareness of the needs of others and the lostness of people around the world. In addition, it would let them participate in answered prayer, which in turn would help build a sense of reality about God and anchor their faith early in life.

In churches where it is easier to pay for programs than it is to pray for the empowerment of programs, more prayer would shift our sense of confidence from our own abilities to His (James 5:16).

Prayer opens our eyes to see God more clearly.

It opens our hearts to hear from Him more directly.

It gives us a greater sense of who we really are—reliant, weak, and needy.

It reminds us of who He really is—the sufficient sustainer and supplier of all we need.

I really think that if we all spent more time practicing the prayers we say we believe in rather than wringing our hands about placing prayer in school, we might have more power in this pagan world than we ever dreamed of.

A WORDLESS CHURCH

Among my many memories from Sunday school, the times we spent singing the gospel message from the "Wordless Book" have been indelibly etched in my mind. To this day, decades later, I can lift a rousing rendition of the song.

The book we sang from had large cardboard pages, each one representing a portion of the gospel message. There was a dark page for sin, a red page for the blood of Christ, a white page for the promise of being forgiven and made as clean as snow, a gold page for the streets of heaven, and a green page for spiritual growth.

It was a wonderful message that left a wonderful memory.

I haven't seen a "Wordless Book" in some time, but it struck me recently that in America we are now seeing a "wordless church." The Word of God seems less eminent, less obvious, and less central to our late twentieth-century brand of Christianity.

Today, fewer of us bring our Bibles to church. That may have something to do with the fact that the congregational reading of Scripture—once considered a community recognition and celebration of the significance of the Word of God—has been eliminated from many of our services.

The trend may also have something to do with the fact that some preachers who wish to appeal to seekers and marginal church attendees now serve sermons "lite" on Sunday. They assume that Bible exposition may be too heavy or too offensive. Their messages sound more like values lectures, with an occasional tip of the hat to Scripture. In addition, it may have something to do with the fact that small-group Bible studies often spend more time studying some book about parenting, the marketplace, retirement, or other contemporary issues rather than the timeless Word of God.

The preeminence of the Word suffers today because too many of us have turned from Scripture to seek healing through therapeutic ministries. Many of these ministries merely echo secular theories, with no reference or adherence to the principles of God's Word.

Have we forgotten the value of God's Word—as an instrument of healing as well as a reminder of our personal responsibility? God's Word, when energized by the work of the Holy Spirit, is our only real hope for effective long-term change in our lives.

We should not, of course, forget that God has given some of His people special gifts of wisdom and insight for helping those with deep inner hurts. The point is that we must not ignore the place, power, and preeminence of the Word of God in the healing process. It not only heals but also guides us toward a productive relationship with God.

What would an increasingly wordless church look like?

It would be a community more committed horizontally to relationships between people than vertically, to its relationship with the triune God.

It would be less driven by dogma and more driven by experience and emotions.

It would be more tolerant of sin and less ready to maintain a clear line between what is right and what is wrong.

It would concentrate more upon pragmatics than upon principle.

Its people would reflect an increasing ignorance of the biblical information that undergirds truth.

It would be a church bonded to its past, its programs, its pastor, and its prominence rather than to its Savior, the head of the church.

It would be a church prone to pride and impurity.

God's Word, however, is indispensable. It is the only authoritative source of our knowledge of Him in His fullness. It convicts us when necessary; it comforts, calms, and compels us to consecrated living. A Word-oriented church produces a community of believers whose lives radiate the qualitative results of righteousness, results that offer undeniable proof of our faith and of our Lord.

A wordless book can make a powerful statement, but a wordless church has lost its message. It has the form of godliness without the power.

Word-filled churches begin with Word-filled parishioners—people who declare with the psalmist, "Oh how I love your law! It is my meditation all the day . . . How sweet are your words to my taste, sweeter than honey to my mouth!" (Psalm 119:97, 103).

Recently my former secretary, Betty McIntyre, sent me a card with this clip enclosed: "Although there are plenty of exceptions, the data shows that middle age is the very best time of life . . . When looking at the total U.S. population, the best year is 50. You don't have to deal with the aches and pains of old age or the anxieties of youth: Is anyone going to love me? Will I ever get my career off the ground? . . . You're healthy, you're productive, you have enough money to do some of the things you like to do . . . Mid-life is the 'it' you've been working toward. You can turn your attention toward being rather than becoming."

The occasion for her kindness was that I, of all people, had turned 50.

I knew it happened to others, but why did it have to happen to me? Now here I am, standing at that threshold of life where I can no longer fool myself. I keep asking myself, *What's this 30-year-old guy doing in this 50-year-old body?* But there is no denying the fact that I really was born in 1944. To add insult to injury, the savage folk from the American Association of Retired Persons now welcome me to pay their dues and take advantage of the benefits of being a senior citizen.

I am aware that this is the middle season of my life because I am smack-dab between my parents and my kids. My dad is healthy at 83, and my youngest child has just turned 21.

As I phased out of my middle-age pity party, I found myself spending time in serious reflection about life in general and about my own life in particular. When we need a benchmark to measure our activities, we often check to see what time it is. When time seems short, we tend to get more focused on the task.

Given where the hands are on my biological clock, it is becoming increasingly important that I maximize my life for God's glory and gain. Heaven seems closer now, and that ultimate divine compliment more compelling. I find myself seeking more jealously to live in a way that I might hear from Him, "Well done, thou good and faithful servant."

I also find myself increasingly disenchanted with the pace and busyness of my life. Those of us who fish know that when you throw a lure toward the shore and reel it back in quickly, it skims across the surface of the water. The slower you reel the lure toward the boat, the deeper it goes. I find myself longing for a slower, more focused, deepening experience, not only with life, but with my Lord—the one who has made my life worthwhile to this point.

Being 50 forces me to think about what I have to give the generation that is coming behind me. Will I be able only to mentor them in how to do life and ministry, or do I have enough depth, insight, and wisdom to help them get beyond doing to becoming?

Eternity looms larger for me now. Having experienced many of life's joys and privileges, I find a deeper, fuller longing in my heart for the experience that I was built and redeemed for.

I am beginning to believe that memories are more important than I had once thought. And that life is about building memories in the hearts of our spouse, children, friends, and associates. I find myself wanting to cast a good and constructive shadow through their minds. I wonder what kind of legacy I'll leave.

My dad used to say, "Friends are the greatest treasure in life." He is right. Again.

There was a time when my life was far too fast, when I was too busy gaining on my dreams to properly value my friends.

Not anymore. Those few who have loved and accepted me through the years regardless of my several faults are great treasures indeed.

I am learning that very few things are really important. Only things like truth, a clear conscience, laughter, giving, serving, and a faithful dog ultimately count.

A quieter, more reflective life. More time to read and grow. The love of my wife, Martie. Deeper intimacy with Christ. These are what occupy my dreams and desires these days.

I find myself often thinking about that little phrase that used to be so common among God's people, "Only one life 'twill soon be past, only what's done for Christ will last."

Perhaps the psalmist was somewhere near my time of life when he prayed, "Teach us to number our days that we may get a heart of wisdom" (Psalm 90:12).

AMERICA'S TOUGHEST JOB

Who has the toughest job in the country?

Somewhere on the list, we need to include your pastor. There is little doubt that pastoring today is tougher than ever before.

It's tougher because technology has brought stellar preachers into our cars and living rooms through radio, TV, and videocassettes. There was a day when most of us thought our pastor was a great preacher because we had never heard anyone else. Now your pastor may step out of the pulpit on Sunday only to hear people in the foyer praising someone else's Friday broadcast.

Pastoring is tougher because people are more distracted. There was a time when an evangelistic crusade or missionary conference would fill a church for a week or even two. In those days, of course, the town calendar had only two events: the revival meeting and the circus. Sometimes you couldn't tell the difference.

Today people have more obligations and outside interests. These hectic schedules often leave them too exhausted for special church activities.

Pastoring is tougher because of our culture's consumer mindset. Once, the work ethic prevailed in America. People went to church asking, "What can I do?" Today we ask, "Do I like this preacher? Do I like the music? Is the youth program good for my children? Do I like the feel of this place?" Few people enter church saying, "How can I contribute to the work of Christ here?"

Pastoring is tougher because expectations are higher and commitment is lower. Discipleship often becomes a disposable commodity, something to toss out if it threatens comfort and convenience.

Granted, pastors don't always make the job easier. Some are dreadfully insecure; others seem arrogant. They may appear overly sensitive at times or tragically insensitive. Pastors find it tough to balance the priorities of family, study, outreach, and care. And sometimes they don't handle the stress well.

Unfortunately, pastors bring all of their humanity to the task of ministry. This is not to deny that their lives should be exemplary. They must! Pastors need to recognize that they will either be examples or excuses for their flock. But their high profile often magnifies weaknesses and camouflages strengths. Even as they seek to be exemplary (1 Timothy 3:1–7), failures will inevitably show.

This is where the congregation can contribute a much-needed spiritual quality: forbearance. When forbearance is added to the formula of pastor plus people, the result is a strong and effective ministry for Jesus Christ.

"Let your forbearing spirit be known to all men," the apostle Paul wrote (Philippians 4:5 ASV). Forbearance is the opposite of rigidity. It is a capacity for tolerance. It is the application of mercy and grace in the face of human frailty.

Some things cannot be tolerated in pastoral leadership: immorality, heresy, dishonesty, slothfulness. But the usual warts of life—and we all have them—must be bathed in the grace of forbearance. First Peter 5 identifies pastors as the under-shepherds of Christ, not Christ Himself. Perfection should not be demanded, not even perfection minus a weakness or two.

Pastors are real people. We rightly expect them to be a bit farther down the road to spiritual maturity than we are, but as we follow them on that road, we will notice that they, like us, bear the scars of the pilgrimage.

If we love the cause of Christ, we would do well to celebrate the strengths of our pastors and seek ways to encourage and affirm their ministry. And in their weakness give them the "elbow room" of forbearance.

Many of us pray for revival. We long for the Spirit's power to transform our churches and make them more effective for the cause of Christ. One of the necessary ingredients for revival is repentance. For some of us, repentance may involve our attitude toward our pastor. The kingdom of Christ is far too strategic for us to spend our time undercutting the under-shepherds.

The Lord gave me the joy of serving as a pastor for seventeen years before He planted me in this corner of His vineyard. My years in the pastorate were fulfilling and rewarding, largely because of congregations who cared for us with a forbearing spirit. No pastor is perfect—I certainly wasn't. But the Christ we serve is. That fact should make us willing to accept one another and, arm in arm, crash the gates of hell.

THE DREAMS WE DREAM,
THE CHOICES WE MAKE

"Our lives are not made by the dreams we dream but by the choices we make." My friend dropped the statement in passing, but its significance stuck in my mind.

We all have dreams—dreams of family, friends, happiness, success, peace, prosperity, and productivity. We dream and hope, wondering if life will be good to us. Unfortunately, dreams aren't the stuff life is made of; choices are what count.

As a boy, I thought my Lionel train set seemed as big as life. The intricate layout allowed me to construct a scenario of travel and trade that would delight any tourist or shipper.

As the plan unfolded, with me at the throttle, the switch tracks were the key. With the press of a button, I could alter the course of the trains and change the whole scheme. Ultimately, I could get a train moving down a track in the opposite direction.

Choices are the switch tracks of life. You and I are at the throttle; life stretches before us. If we throw the switch, life takes a turn. What we do today is the product of all the choices we have made.

And regardless of how bad things are around us, our sovereignty of choice remains. We are never ultimately victims of circumstance.

Dietrich Bonhoeffer, the German theologian, having been stripped of his degrees, family, library, work, and dignity, stood naked before his Nazi accusers and said that though they had taken everything from him, one thing they could not take. That was his ability to choose in that moment how he would respond to them. Choice, one of life's greatest privileges, is always and only ours.

I have always wanted life to be simple, with choices that are clearly good or clearly bad. My idealism has not been rewarded. Life is complex. There are rotten choices, bad choices, and average choices.

We have all fallen into the trap of average choices. It's that great swamp of mediocrity where the "everyone does it" crowd pitches their tents—the campground of "Nothing in the Bible says it's wrong" and "A lot of people do worse."

God speaks clearly about choices when He directs us to "approve the things that are excellent," literally, "put excellent things to the test" (Philippians 1:10 NASB). He calls us to go beyond average, beyond even good, to the choices marked excellent.

Granted, restricting our lives to excellence is challenging. We may have to go alone. We may have to yield comfort, cash, or convenience, but the gain is worth it.

We are to choose excellence "so that you may approve what is excellent, and so be pure and blameless for the day of Christ, filled with the fruit of righteousness that comes through Jesus Christ, to the glory and praise of God" (Philippians 1:10–11).

Excellence brings purity. There is nothing better in life than the pleasure of not having to look over your shoulder to see if someone saw or heard what you did. Purity sets us free from the haunting shadow that "I might get caught."

Excellence brings productivity. Whenever people talk of my predecessor, Dr. Sweeting, they speak most often of his character, marked by grace, wisdom, and courage. How will others talk of what we do or the quality of our lives? The fruits of righteousness grow on lives committed to excellent choices.

Excellence brings purpose. A life of purpose brings glory to God, the reason for our redemption (1 Corinthians 6:19–20).

What makes a choice excellent? Love, knowledge, and a discerning application of the two. "And it is my prayer that your love may abound more and more, with knowledge and all discernment, so that you may approve what is excellent, and so be pure and blameless for the day of Christ (Philippians 1:9–10).

Love chooses what is best for others, not what is best for me. Knowledge guides every choice by the clear principles of the Word of God.

In my years of pastoral counseling, I don't recall talking to anyone with a problem resulting from a commitment to excellent choices. In fact, most cases revealed that the person had somewhere thrown a switch for selfishness instead of love or for self-will instead of submission to God's Word.

When we do what is best for others according to the direction of God's Word, excellence is the product: excellent dads, moms, children, pastors, and employees. Excellent living.

For our lives are not made by the dreams we dream, but by the choices we make.

LOCAL HERO

Heroes are made, not born. Unless, that is, you are a dad. When it comes to being heroes, dads have an edge. They start out as heroes. Their only task is to stay that way. A dad's hero status is no insignificant privilege. Good heroes are in short supply.

When I was young, heroes seemed to earn their respect. In addition to my dad, my heroes were baseball players like Whitey Ford, Mickey Mantle, and Yogi Berra. They never captured headlines because of drugs, womanizing, or gambling. That doesn't necessarily mean they didn't have those problems, just that their hero status remained intact.

Musical heroes dressed and acted like real people. They smiled and sang ballads about love and life. A war hero sat in the White House, and religious celebrities were worth emulating.

It seems that today all the hero slots have been marred. Today's heroes are not necessarily worse people than past heroes—we just know too much about them. Sadly, knowing all we do, we still hold many up as heroes. Young people launch themselves into the same devastating patterns seen in the lives of those they look up to.

In the midst of this atmosphere, dads have the opportunity to be heroes of a different sort, to model a different way of life.

Hero status comes with fatherhood. We don't earn it or accomplish it by some stellar feat. Our children look up to us from day one. Good stewardship requires us to maintain our status as a privilege and enhance it in every way possible.

Our children won't forever yell with admiration, "Mommy, Mommy, Daddy's home!" When we become careless with our children, disenfranchised from their needs, we leave tender, worshipful hearts disappointed, discouraged, and often embittered.

Our children don't expect us to be perfect (the only perfect Father is in heaven). But we who aren't in heaven must preserve a strong role model in the eyes of those God has entrusted to our care. We must make certain commitments.

Humility. Not the doormat variety, but biblical humility that gladly and visibly submits to God and gives Him credit for our accomplishments. To admit we are wrong, without qualification or excuse, displays humility and enhances our standing as local hero.

Loving Mom. A good marriage, one in which Mom and Dad regularly show their love through word and deed, is a child's primary source of security. Martie once whispered to one of our children on her lap, "I love you more than anyone else in the whole wide world." The child replied, "More than you love Daddy? I want you to love Daddy more than anybody else in the world."

Dads who know how to be tender toward their wives are revered by their children.

Time and attention. My children are not particularly impressed with my title or the things I do. They may brag to their friends about Dad once in a while, but when it comes to a personal relationship, only two things impress them: my time and attention.

My busy preacher dad on many occasions set aside all he was doing to take me to Yankee Stadium to watch my heroes play baseball. And I still remember him taking me fishing in the summer.

But time isn't the only thing that impresses children. They need attention as well. Sometimes, even when I take time to be with them, my mind is elsewhere. They say, "Dad, are you listening?" Paying attention is the best compliment you can give someone.

I sometimes remind myself that my children have read none of the books I have written. I don't think they're impressed. But they are impressed when they have my time and attention.

Heroes have impact. We tend to admire our heroes so deeply that we talk, respond, and even act like they do. When I think about the legacy I will leave my children, I wonder if it will be of one willing to bow low before God and others.

Will I inspire my children to love their spouses with Christ's love? Will they know how to give the gift of time and attention to their own children?

Children start by looking up *at* us. My prayer is that my children will find legitimate reasons to look up *to* me.

As scary as fatherhood can be, I like being a dad. It may be my only shot in life at being a hero.

ALONE

I treasure the occasional chance to be alone.

Of course, I love where God has put me: I thoroughly enjoy serving Christ at Moody Bible Institute. And I have a deep and intimate love for each member of my family.

Yet with those loves comes a measure of stress from responsibilities measured in people's lives, the future of Christ's work, the legacy of our family, and, most significantly, eternity.

So I usually welcome those times—in the early morning before the family is up or in the car on my commute—when I am apart and need manage only me.

Yet one recent Sunday, aloneness felt unwelcome and different. I stood in the church foyer after an evening service with nowhere to go and no one to go with. My wife and daughter had taken advantage of Libby's spring break for a well-deserved fling. Joe was away at school; Matt was with friends.

I stopped at a restaurant on the way home. At the table next to mine, two women were having an intense discussion.

I am not an eavesdropper, but I would have had to move to keep from hearing them. One talked desperately of how alone she felt at home. Significantly, she *wasn't* alone. She had a husband—that was the problem.

She felt his only interest in her was external and physical. She longed for eye contact that said, "I care. I'm listening. What do you need? How can I help?"

Despite encouragement from her friend, she would not be comforted. Her despair was deep. She didn't want much—just not to be alone in her home, in her relationship with someone who had promised so much.

A young couple came in, obviously lost in the joys of court-ship. Their eyes fixed on each other as they talked and smiled. They never ran out of steam. They were interested in each other, discovering each other.

I wondered if they would someday feel alone at home.

Then I had a penetrating thought. Though it was interrupted by the arrival of my meal, it wouldn't go away: *Could Martie feel alone in our relationship?*

Neither of us expects to continue to feel what we did in those early days of discovery and anticipation, but I assumed that through the years we had gone beyond first love to something deeper and richer. But I have been wrong before.

I thought of times when Martie and I had talked about my sensitivity to her needs, perspectives, and wants—about listening, and why I sometimes seemed to be looking elsewhere when she was talking.

I comforted myself that our relationship would never be marked by the despair of the woman at the next table. But I renewed my commitment to guarantee that Martie would never feel alone in our home.

As I headed home, I began to wonder why I felt so unsettled about being alone. Then it struck me. I was alone in the place where I shouldn't be alone: at home.

My enjoyment of those early morning times was accompanied by the knowledge that I was not really alone. Martie and the children were sleeping, but they were there.

The Lord moved me to tenderness toward those who are truly alone: widows, widowers, single parents, divorcees, those whose families are far way, those who have no family. Sadly I included lonely husbands, wives, children, and parents—those surrounded by families, yet alone.

I realized that many in the church that night had felt alone. They walked out to empty cars, empty homes, maybe empty restaurant tables. If we're not supposed to be alone at home, we're certainly not supposed to be alone at church. Though it can never replace the intimacy of a home, the church is called to fill the gap.

I thought of a recent message that encouraged lonely people to adopt a family. That advice was good and well meant, but perhaps it was backwards. Those of us who are not alone need to find those who are, reach out, and fold them in.

God said about Adam, "It is not good that the man should be alone" (Genesis 2:18). Yet Adam was not alone: He had God. Shouldn't that have been enough? Evidently not.

Though our relationship with God is paramount, God designed us to need other people as well. I need someone I can see and hold—someone who can hold me, hear me, and to whom I can express who I am and what I'm thinking.

How alone my Savior must have felt. Though surrounded by people, He was rarely understood, and in the end He suffered and died alone.

My aloneness made me love Him more. I knew afresh how deeply He must care for those who are alone.

PART FIVE

TAKE THE HELMET
OF SALVATION

TO TELL THE TRUTH

Mr. Clinton entered the office of president with a promise and a hope. The promise was to have the most ethical administration in history, and his hope was that he would be a Kennedyesque leader who would restore the Camelot days of that era.

After six years into his presidency, both appeared to have vanished.

At the heart of the firestorm that engulfed Washington was the fact that the president lied. As important as his contrite spirit was, the damage was immense.

Evidence indicates that he lied under oath—to Americans, to his family, to his closest friends and advisors—and then asked them to repeat the lie, dragging them into the quagmire of his own demise. I'm reminded of Sir Walter Scott's words, "Oh what a tangled web we weave, when first we practice to deceive."

As unsettling as all of this was, most Americans seemed unconcerned about the lies. Polls indicated that an astounding number of people felt that if the chief guardian of the law lied under oath, it would not be reason for either his resignation or impeachment. Man-on-the-street interviews were full of comments saying in effect, "It's no big deal."

Actually, it *is* a big deal when a leader—or anyone else—lies. Lying destroys truth. When truth is displaced, we lose the ability to trust.

A loss of trust erodes the stability and security that we need in healthy relationships. When truth evaporates and takes trust with it, insecurity and suspicion make the day.

In many ways President Clinton is a man of our times. He was the first president to have grown up in an America where truth is no longer paramount—where the notion prevails that there are no absolutes.

If there are no absolutes, then there is no absolute truth, and everyone's point of view is equally valid, which leaves us to decisions driven by the polls and to a world where spin replaces substance, and the powerful, not the truthful, prevail.

As followers of Christ, we say we claim to be people of the truth. But we often find that lies are handy when we are in a tight spot, when we need to enhance ourselves, or when lying helps advance a dream or desire.

I love coconut—in any shape or form. As a boy I remember finding a bag of moist, sweet shredded coconut in the kitchen cupboard. I ate it all. How was I to know that my mother was planning to use it to bake a cake for dinner that night?

Finding that her cupboard was bare, she queried my sisters and me only to discover that according to our testimony, none of us was guilty.

When my dad, the chief prosecutor of our family, came home, he heard the same testimony. Then, as a last-ditch effort to smoke out the criminal among us, he pulled out his Bible and read from the passage in Revelation that liars are among those who have their place in the lake of fire (21:8).

That did it! I repented, took my punishment, and became permanently sensitized to the importance of the truth.

God's view of lying should bring all of us to our senses.

A lying tongue is included on the list of the six things the Lord hates (Proverbs 6:17). The wisdom writer reminds us that, "Lying lips are an abomination to the Lord, but those who deal faithfully are His delight" (Proverbs 12:22 NASB).

Lying is offensive to God because He is true. There is nothing false in Him. Lying contradicts His very nature and threatens the stability of relationships and the safety and security of society.

Truth-telling should be a distinguishing mark of those of us who are called by His name.

If we spent more time telling the truth than pointing our fingers, then we could demonstrate to a truthless world that we are truth-tellers who can be trusted regardless of the circumstances.

Maybe then they will want to know of the Savior in whom they can fully trust as well.

Elizabeth Barrett Browning's poetic question is vitally relevant to our relationship with Christ. *How* do we love Him? More importantly, *do* we love Him? We dare not rush to answer. The issue is too profound.

Loving Christ is at the heart of what it means to be involved in an authentic relationship with Him. He doesn't want just our heads—or the sterile surrender of a will that has been cajoled, codified, and required to obey Him. Jesus chastised the religious folk of his day for honoring God with their lips while their hearts were far from Him (Matthew 15:7–8). "Do you love me?" was the last question He asked Peter. And to the church at Ephesus, which Revelation 2 says was skilled in good works, Christ issued an injunction that they were to repent from the sin of having left their first love.

It's no small matter that the first and great commandment is "Love the Lord your God" (Matthew 22:37). I admit how embarrassed I am that for years I taught that the essence of loving God is yielding our will. It's not that being yielded is unimportant. It's that yieldedness without affection is the busywork of the kingdom. I agree with John Calvin who insisted that truth is intended to engage our affections, not merely to "flit about in our brains."

As we chatted over coffee, a graduate student in theology asked the ultimate question. "What does it mean to love God?" We discussed such aspects of love as obedience and yieldedness, the meanings of the Greek word *love*, and felt pretty good having theologized our way through the issue.

Yet if the weeping woman of Luke 7, whom Jesus had forgiven much, had pulled up a chair, we would have heard a different spin.

She, who had wet Jesus' feet with her tears and wiped them with her hair, would have spoken of affection and adoration, of risky and radical actions that express a heart of unquenchable gratitude, of being once a burdened, maligned sinner but now set free, of finding Someone who truly cared for her, and that she loved Him for it. She would have said in certain terms that loving Christ is not an item on our list of what we ought to do, but a response to the wonderful things He has done. She would have spoken with an intensity and passion that is often absent in the detached analysis we Bible boomers bring to the discussion.

But then, Christ had radically touched her. She had been forgiven much. As Christ noted, there is a direct correlation between being forgiven much and loving much. That may be why many of us struggle to ignite in our hearts an adoring, life-changing love for Christ. Most of us feel pretty good about ourselves, which makes it tough to feel that we are among the "forgiven much."

I periodically preach at the Brooklyn Tabernacle in New York City. Many of the members there have been saved out of the bowels of Brooklyn. They tell stories of redemption from crack abuse, prostitution, and lives of crime.

I have to tell you that I leave there feeling somewhat cheated. It's not that I want the struggles of the residual baggage of their sin. It's that they love Jesus Christ in a special way. They weep with joy at what He has done for them. They live to gratefully express their love to Him.

I accepted Christ at age 6. So I was redeemed from things like biting my sister and not picking up my room. For people like me, Christianity is more easily a lifestyle than a heartstyle. Being a third-generation follower, I struggle to feel forgiven much. My guess is that the theology student was also a lifer with Jesus. Otherwise he may not have had to ask what it means to love Christ.

However, reality insists that I, too, am among the "forgiven much." It is the worst stroke of self-deceit to assume otherwise.

Even my best accomplishments are like filthy rags in the blazing purity of His holy presence. Where might greed, lust, or self-absorption have taken me had not His amazing grace reached my wretchedness at such an early age?

When I think about who I really am—and what might have been—I find that my heart awakens to the adoration and affection that my Savior deserves.

A LEGACY WORTH LEAVING

I have a friend who collects epitaphs from gravestones. Some are unbelievably funny, and others have weight and significance. Our interest in summarizing life in a few clipped phrases says something about our need to bring closure in a terse and memorable way.

A letter arrived from a woman in Detroit. Mary wrote to tell me her dad had passed away. I loved her dad. He was a quiet, deep man whose life I held in the highest regard. It was easy to respect Larry. Most who knew him felt the same way.

Larry and his wife moved to Louisville to retire near one of their married daughters. Over a period of time, three of his daughters and their husbands moved to live near them. As one of the sons-in-law said, Larry was so special that he wanted his four children to grow up knowing him. Larry died of a cancerous brain tumor. As he became ill, the men cared for him. They counted him their best friend.

Mary wrote that even though her dad became quite immobile toward the end, he still knelt before God in prayer each night. It took two people to get him back on his feet again and into bed. Though he knew little else, he still knew his Savior.

Larry had walked the streets of Detroit during the riots of the 1960s, ministering to those who were injured. His love for people, especially the downcast, led him to encourage Mary to take a job teaching in the inner city sixteen years ago.

He never had a high profile, at least not with men. But Larry had an enviable love for Christ and others that contagiously showed. Mary writes, "I remember him as an energetic man who had no fear to do what was right in the eyes of God."

What struck me in the letter was what a friend said at the funeral. "It hurts so much because the world has lost a righteous man, and that is no small thing."

I have often wondered what they will say about me when I am gone. What friends and family say is a commentary on the legacy we leave behind. Most of us have been so busy building a life that we have forgotten that life is really about building a legacy.

To watch most of us, you would think we are hoping they will say something about our busyness, our accumulation of stacks of stuff, our travels, our golf, our detailed knowledge of every sport statistic known to man, or our computer wizardry. It's a commentary on our times that bodybuilding gets higher billing these days than legacy building.

Some of us do far better in growing a career than a legacy. As my friend Howard Hendricks says, "You spend your life climbing the ladder of success only to find that when you reach the top, it is leaning against the wrong wall."

Think of standing at the threshold of eternity and looking back at your life. What would you like the spin to be? What would the sound bites say?

Would the phrases surround words like *godly, wise, caring, compassionate, honest, courageous,* and *Christlike?* Would they talk about how much we had loved our spouses and made our children a priority? Would they have noticed that we loved Christ more than anything else in life—that we had lived a life that reflected all we said we believed?

Are any of us living a life that is so solidly compelling that our kids want to be sure that our grandchildren don't miss letting us rub off on them?

Mary's letter reminds me that my life needs to be about giving those who are left behind the summary of a life whose memories cast a long, powerfully positive shadow over the generations to come.

I'd give anything if they could say of me, "It hurts because the world has lost a righteous man, and that's no small thing."

And that may be what I have to give—*anything* that gets in the way of my being a righteous man who, as Mary said, "had no fear to do what was right in the eyes of God."

In my book that's a legacy worth leaving—and worth living for.

Why is it that the essentials of our walk with Christ seem so difficult for us? While we know that regular Bible reading, significant seasons of prayer, and the expression of gratitude, praise, submissiveness, and servanthood are certainly important, they remain commodities of our Christianity that are often talked about yet rarely practiced. Because of this, we remain less than what God hopes for, and we experience far less than He is willing to provide.

We have many reasons these essentials find such sparse expression in our lives. We say that because they are so important, Satan launches his assault on these areas first. In a twisted way we blame our failure on his supremacy in the very arena where we are strengthened for the warfare. More often we are just tired of trying and failing. After repeated attempts to inculcate these habits, we slip back into life as usual. And, as we do with New Year's resolutions, we become cynical about our good intentions.

It probably has not crossed our minds that these basic behaviors were not intended to be the tasks of our faith. If that is all they are, then it's no wonder that left to ourselves we lack the initiative to sustain them. No one likes doing chores.

These are spontaneous responses. They are not territories to be conquered only by the highly disciplined, super-spiritual among us. They are the expressions of those who realize something profound about themselves. What stimulates these essential expressions is the realization that we are frail, and we desperately need Him.

Seeing ourselves as frail and needy is not easy. We are trained to think well of ourselves and to believe that we are strong and sufficient. Any sense of weakness is shunned and denied. We masquerade our neediness with piles of accumulated stuff and with defense mechanisms that keep out intruders who would unveil our true condition.

Often the things that God has provided for us get in the way of our seeing what we really are at the core. Some of us are greatly gifted. Others have talents galore. Some have power and platforms of influence. Most of us have a measure of good health that gives us strength and energy. Some have been blessed with financial resources that are beyond our needs. It's little wonder that we find it difficult to believe that we are desperately needy. It seems to escape us that all we have comes from God. We are apt to forget that without the blessing of God on these gifts, they are of no value.

David, who as king had all he needed to feel self-sufficient, had an unusual perspective on life. In Psalm 23, he saw himself as a lamb and God as his shepherd.

There could be no clearer picture of a useful yet totally reliant life than that of sheep in relationship to their shepherd. This perspective is the reason why David was known as a man after God's own heart. It gives insight as well into why he penned so many hymns that resound with expressions of his need and exuberant strains of reliance, praise, adoration, and submission to the Shepherd of his life.

Unlike David, we tend not to be so honest about ourselves. We think more highly of ourselves than we ought (Romans12:3). We really are in need of Him, and spiritual sanity insists that we recognize our need to be completely and fully reliant on Him.

We really need God. We must be convinced of our frailty and His strength. He is willing to pour the fullness of His strength into our weakness.

When we willingly admit how dependent we are, then prayer, gratitude, submission, and the other essentials will be normative, ongoing responses. Not projects, but products of a realistic view of who we are, who He is, and how profound a privilege it is to be the recipients of His fullness.

Our hearts need to resonate with the psalmist who proclaims, "Whom have I in heaven but you? And there is nothing on earth that I desire besides you. My flesh and my heart may fail, but God is the strength of my heart and my portion forever" (Psalm 73:25–26).

Childhood heroes etch their impressions deep within our hearts. In fact, with time they usually take on a life of their own—moving from memory to myth.

It's been like that for most of my life with Mickey Mantle—until his life-style off the field eroded both the myth and the memory.

You can imagine my surprise when Bobby Richardson, former teammate of the Mick, related in the *Los Angeles Times* that just a few days before his death, Mantle told him that he had accepted Christ as his personal Savior. I was thrilled. Just think—I might finally get to meet him . . . in heaven.

As a boy I had often waited outside the players' exit to Yankee Stadium, hoping to see Mantle up close. *It's too bad we won't care about autographs in heaven,* I thought. *Maybe I could have gotten one after all.*

Seriously, my mind traveled down several paths when I heard the good news. My thoughts were loaded with application far beyond the life and death of my hero.

Bobby Richardson, who officiated at Mantle's funeral, related to me that he has received more than three hundred letters from people who said they had been praying for Mickey in the last months of his life—praying that God would bring individuals around him to tell him the good news.

That prayer was good news in and of itself. My guess is that most of us wrote Mantle off a long time ago and greeted the news of his demise with a measure of, "Well, that's what you get when you drink your way through life."

I am continually amazed at how long we are on consternation and how short we are on compassion. When was the last time you prayed intensely through the headlines of your daily newspaper for the souls and needs of those in trouble? Trouble has a way of softening the hearts of even the most public of people.

Paul Azinger relates that he did not think beyond the pursuit of temporal success until—at the height of his professional golf career—he heard that he had cancer. He tells how the words that the chaplain of the golf tour had said so often started to ring true to him: "We think that we are in the land of the living headed for the land of the dying, when in reality we are in the land of the dying headed for the land of the living." As the "Zinger" came to grips with these words, he also came to grips with his need for a Savior.

I thought as well that Mickey Mantle's story proves once more that at the end of life, fame, fortune, and the "good life" are not nearly enough. As Christ stated so clearly, "For what does it profit a man to gain the whole world and forfeit his life? For what can a man give in return for his life?" (Mark 8:36–37). Christ's story of a mega-mover in the marketplace, who prospered so much that he had to tear down his barns to build bigger ones, concludes with the note that he was a fool because he ignored eternity (Luke 12:16–21). As Mickey Mantle discovered, what he truly needed for life was the sufficient grace of God to guarantee life in the world to come.

I thought as well how this marvelous grace so patiently waits, ready to receive anyone at any time. Think of the fact that God, who had been ignored and offended for a lifetime, stood without rage at the edge of eternity offering mercy and grace to Mantle's repentant heart.

Richardson's wife knelt by Mickey's chair a few days before he went home to be with the Lord, asking him how he knew for sure that he had been born again. Mantle recited, "For God so loved the world that he gave his only begotten Son, that whosoever believeth in him should not perish, but have everlasting life" (John 3:16 KJV). I found myself marveling again at how profoundly simple the offer of salvation is, particularly given the fact that the stakes are so high.

Toward the end, Mantle confidently told his doctors, "I'm ready to go now." I thought of what a "blessed assurance" Jesus is when it is time to step over the threshold.

I learned a lot about baseball from watching Mickey Mantle execute the game. He thrilled me often as he cleared the fences with his powerful swing. But I never thought that my boyhood hero would thrill me afresh about the marvelous grace of God. God is good!

I t may be true that on most nights before Christmas, no one is stirring—not even a mouse. But that certainly was not the case on that first Christmas night.

The birth of Christ was a shot heard from the throne room of God to the darkest dens of the subterranean halls of hell. It launched hell's most frantic assault, with ramifications that reach far beyond that starry night.

Let me explain.

For most people, Christmas is wrapped in glorious packages of ribbons, wreaths, lights, bells, and good cheer. If we did not know better, we would simply see December 25 as marking the arrival of one who lived such a unique and interesting life that His presence revolutionized the world and shaped Western culture for two thousand years.

For those of us who know the Christ of Christmas, the day is far deeper and richer than that. It's the Incarnation, God become man. It's redemption. We celebrate with heartwarming carols and majestic proclamations of the joy of Jesus Christ, with church pageants and living Christmas trees.

But underneath it all, there lays a dark side. At the birth of Jesus Christ, something striking and significant that most of us miss.

In a very real sense, hell itself broke loose when Christ was born. As the heavens burst with a blaze of the angelic presence, the doors of darkness opened and the evil forces of night moved across the landscape like an impending fog.

The Light of the World had been born, and the darkness was bent on its annihilation.

In the book of Revelation, the apostle John unveils a sobering scenario about the spiritual underworld at this moment. He writes concerning the nation Israel: "A woman clothed with the sun, with the moon under her feet, and on her head a crown of twelve stars [appeared]. She was pregnant and was crying out in birth pains and the agony of giving birth. And another sign appeared in heaven: behold a great red dragon . . . The dragon stood before the woman who was about to give birth, so that when she bore her child he might devour it" (Revelation 12:1–4).

The attack began from our Lord's earliest moments on earth—from King Herod's decree to slaughter every male infant in Bethlehem to opposition from Christ's own family to the threats from the religious and political systems of the day.

It culminated with Satan's finest hour, when the Messiah, the Creator of the world, the God of the universe, hung on a cross, killed by hands that had become tools for Satan's trade.

It is easy for us to assume that what we see is all there is. It is easy to assume that the world is fundamentally good and right, the source of peace, pleasure, and comfort. Even we Christians spend most of our time focusing on the topside of redemption, on the good things that we have in Jesus Christ.

Yet if we are going to be realistic and fully aware of all that we are up against, we must remember the massive power of the kingdom of hell. Our adversary is still bent on the destruction of Christ and His cause.

Though we must take note of the dark side, Christmas rises as God's dawn against the night. Satan sought to destroy the Messiah, and for three days after His death celebrated with all the legions of the fallen. Then the sovereign power of God touched the tomb, and the dawn eclipsed the night.

Christmas is about victory won against the power of the night. Celebrating Christmas means celebrating Christ's victory, not only two thousand years ago but also in the daily circumstances of our lives. Every time we say no to Satan and stand against temptation and bring the power of Christ's glory against the onslaught of our adversary, we celebrate what Christmas is really about.

Christmas reminds us that the darkness could not restrain the emerging dawn. And it assures us that one day Satan will be ultimately and finally defeated. In that day we will eternally celebrate the Messiah from the manger with resounding anthems of, "Worthy is the Lamb who was slain, to receive power and wealth and wisdom and might and honor and glory and blessing! . . . To him who sits on the throne and to the Lamb be blessing and honor and glory and might forever and ever!" (Revelation 5:12–13).

TIME AND ETERNITY

Any time we want to describe something as really dangerous, we usually attach *ism* to the end. With a few exceptions, *isms* refer to things we dislike or fear: racism, communism, liberalism, conservatism.

Over the past thirty years, *isms* such as sensualism, hedonism, pluralism, relativism, existentialism, narcissism, and materialism have become the driving forces in our godless culture. We who are committed to biblical values understand the debilitating effect of these problems, for individuals and for society.

There is, however, an *ism* that few of us talk about. It may well be the most dangerous of all: *temporalism.* Temporalism means seeing all of life through this brief window of time, as if today is all that really matters. Temporalism gives no thought to eternity or even to the long-term implications of our actions. Temporalism lives by the edict of now.

But in the light of eternity, this present life, this brief flicker called time, is insignificantly small. We must remember that we are not merely people of now. Life finds its meaning and significance in the context of eternity.

For those of us who know Christ, who have had hell canceled and heaven guaranteed, eternity dramatically alters our view of others. The people I live with, work with, associate with, and even meet casually all need to be seen in light of eternity. An eternalist will seek to explain the reality of Christ to those who have not yet considered His relevance to their eternity.

Eternity also reorders our view of possessions. An eternalist asks, "How can I use all that I have to enhance eternity?" That might mean using a home to exercise hospitality, build friendships, and hold Bible studies. We realize that eternities can be changed through the wise use of our material resources.

Temporalists, on the other hand, will be tempted to hoard their possessions. Because this life is all that they have, they fear losing any of it.

To stretch us beyond time, Christ told the story of a rich man who had to build bigger barns to hold his resources. God said, "Fool! This night your soul is required of you, and the things you have prepared, whose will they be?" (Luke 12:20). Christ made the same point when He asked, "What will it profit a man if he gains the whole world and forfeits his life?" (Matthew 16:26).

Eternalists also view pleasure and passion in a broader sense. They can enjoy good things as temporary gifts from their eternal Father, but they don't build their lives on them. They don't want anything to seduce them from love and loyalty to God.

The essence of Christianity is eternal. We belong to Christ, He is eternal, and He is taking us to His eternal home. All of life can be lived in the light of that marvelous reality.

Escaping temporalism would be much easier if the church had a clearer perspective on eternity. Unfortunately, much of our church talk and church work has been clouded by temporalism.

With rising needs in our rapidly decaying society, we have compelling reasons to be involved in causes of justice and compassion. But if we labor outside the context of eternity, we have nothing but temporal gain. As a friend of mine who heads a relief agency says, "Ultimately, it doesn't make a lot of difference if you give people a full stomach without also helping them to receive a full eternity."

Christians are certainly free to enjoy a lot of things that aren't anchored in a Bible verse. Yet many of our church activities have little eternal significance. Even preaching has become temporal. Instead of being grounded in eternal truths and emphasizing eternal rewards, sermons often are little more than pragmatic lessons on what works best in this present life.

I'm thankful that God promises us more than the here and now. As Paul wrote, all of creation, including our bodies, groans under the penalty of our fallenness and anxiously awaits the fullness of our redemption (Romans 8:22–23).

Eternity means a bigger, better day to come. A day—no—a forever of unhindered fellowship, intimacy, joy, and pleasure in the presence of God. If we didn't have an eternity like that, life here would be stained and strained by despair. Life on this planet is just too tough if this is all there is.

Thankfully, in Christ this is not all there is. He who loves us and gave Himself for us is now preparing a better place for us. "If I go and prepare a place for you," He promised, "I will come again and will take you to myself, that where I am you may be also (John 14:3).

LONGING FOR HOME

I'm on the tail end of several intensive weeks of ministry. I've traveled hundreds of miles, met scores of God's people, and spent many happy hours teaching His Word. But despite the excitement of the past weeks, I find myself longing for home—for our place and for Martie and Matt.

Interesting, isn't it, how much of life is linked to longings. As children, we longed for Christmas, for the ball game Dad promised to take us to, for summer vacation. As we grew older, our longings changed: for that next date, for marriage, for retirement, or even a quiet morning at home with a cup of Colombian coffee and our favorite newspaper.

Unfortunately, our longings sometimes leak over the boundaries of what is right and reasonable. God's Word calls that lust. These misguided longings often lead to patterns and habits that our adversary then uses to distort, diminish, and destroy us.

Some of us see our longings as enemies. We know how easily they can drag us into the dark alleys of this world, where the thugs of Beelzebub lurk. So we try to eliminate our passions. If somehow we could only be more stoic, we think, then we would be more spiritual.

Nothing could be further from the truth. We were built as people of passion.

In the beginning, our passions pointed us in all the right directions, for fulfillment in all the right things. Adam and Eve enjoyed a phenomenally fulfilling relationship with the Creator and with all creation. They were made in the image of God; they were built for Him. But then sin entered human history, leaving us spiritually dead and separated from God. Stripped of His presence and power, our longing souls were sent into a godless environment searching for something that would fill the vacuum.

Those who have lost a spouse, a child, or an intimate friend know the longing for what is lost. No matter how busy we get, no matter how many things we acquire, nothing really satisfies that longing.

So it is with this lost relationship with God. Having lost what we were built for and the only source of true meaning and fulfill-ment, our passions flee to a myriad of lesser and sometimes lurid longings. Yet we find no ultimate satisfaction.

The creation narrative reveals three points of linkage for the first human pair. They were first and foremost linked to God and then to the material order and to each other. Any break in these linkages creates normal and often healthy longings in our lives. Through sin we have lost our linkage to God, the primal longing of our hearts. That is why all our lesser longings, even the best ones, can never provide experiences that fully satisfy.

This is what makes redemption so absolutely wonderful. It reconnects us to the source of ultimate satisfaction. Our longings find basic fulfillment in God—in part now and in fullness through eternity when we reach home.

But many of us, even though we've been redeemed, have not trained our souls in this redemptive privilege. Not focusing our passions on Him, we long for that which is less. That's why so much of our life, even in the best of times, seems so unsatisfying.

Our hearts should beat with the passion of the psalmist who declared, "As a deer pants for flowing streams, so pants my soul for you, O God. My soul thirsts for God, for the living God. When shall I come and appear before God?" (Psalm 42:1–2).

The Scriptures describe the issues that constantly work against our passion for God: material surplus (Deuteronomy 6:10–12; 8:10–18), self-absorption (Philippians 3:4–14), ritualized Christi-anity (Revelation 2:1–7), and just plain sin (Genesis 3:1–11). But when we repent and refocus our longing for God, the flame warms our hearts again.

As that longing revives, it draws us onward and homeward. Like a compelling magnetic force, it pulls our souls toward heaven. Those of us who know the wonderful grace of redemption look forward to an eternity with God, when all things will be made new, when all our longings will at last find ultimate and final satisfaction.

But even on the way home, we can know a measure of that satisfaction–through meaningful worship, submission, and unhindered fellowship with our Savior and Friend. There is no satisfaction on this side that compares to feeling the touch of His hand on our hearts and sensing His Spirit within us.

No wonder that the hymn writer exclaims, "Hallelujah! I have found Him whom my soul so long has craved! Jesus satisfies my longings—through His blood I now am saved."

GO-CARTS AND BUMPER CARS

Recently, my son Matt, my nephew, and I went out for an evening of go-carting. As I was whizzing around the track, trying desperately to catch up with those two light-bodied, limber guys, I was struck by the futility of going in circles and cutting off everyone who got in the way.

A lot like life, I thought.

Then I found myself reflecting on a similar, more brutal form of entertainment: bumper cars.

In my affinity for bumper cars, I've discovered that they are driven by two kinds of people. The aggressive ones bump and bang everyone within range. They don't feel successful unless they have plowed as many people into the sideboards as the time has allowed.

The other kind shrinks from the conflict, seeking to avoid the drivers with that killer look in their eyes.

I think a lot of us tend to live out our Christianity in ways that resemble the go-cart and bumper car drivers of our world. Some of us seem content simply to follow a track going nowhere, hoping to finish first on the heap of others who live only for personal glory and self-fulfillment regardless of what happens to friend or foe in the process.

Then there are those who must think there is some spiritual merit to bumping and banging brothers and sisters in Christ, seemingly void of any compassion. Others of us exercise our Christianity in passive avoidance, simply trying to stay out of everybody's way. We don't go anywhere or do anything significant; we just stay out of trouble.

None of these approaches is reflective of the progressive productive sense of our calling in Christ. The essence of authentic

Christianity is the pursuit of a goal. Together, arm in arm, heart to heart, we are called to *get someplace* for God.

For instance, God has left clusters of us Christians on this planet to carry out the Great Commission. He expects us to display the light in our dark generation in such compelling ways that we call people to discipleship, lead them in baptism, and train them to do all that Christ has commanded (Matthew 28:18–20).

In the process of carrying out the Great Commission, we have been assigned the wonderful privilege of glorifying God in our bodies (1 Corinthians 6:19–20). This privilege of reflecting the image of the invisible God through our visible actions and attitudes is what motivated the apostle Paul: "That . . . now as always Christ will be honored in my body, whether by life or by death" (Philippians 1:20).

As followers of Christ, we have many wonderful and productive places to go—in terms of rearing godly families, in expressing a life-changing faith within a pagan culture, and in taking the healing power of Christ to the broken and oppressed.

Perhaps our problem is that we have forgotten that we are a people with a purpose. If we forget our destination, it's easy to slip into the bumper-car mentality and live our lives like a demolition derby. "Do not use your freedom as an opportunity for the flesh," Paul warned. "But through love serve one another . . . If you bite and devour one another, watch out that you are not consumed by one another" (Galatians 5:13, 15).

When our family goes on vacation, we climb into the car with a clear destination in mind. Our goal is to get there as safely and quickly as possible. That means I try to avoid conflict with other cars. I stay out of the way of troublemakers—the lane-jumpers, the creepers, the ones who race down the shoulder to cut in on the waiting lines of traffic. I focus on the business of getting to the final landing spot.

Wanting to reach our destination safely and quickly, I also try to obey the rules of the road. It makes little sense wasting time and money on the shoulder, chatting with the freeway's finest, if we're really about the business of getting there.

At the end of his life, Paul was able to say with confidence, "I have fought the good fight, I have finished the race, I have kept the faith" (2 Timothy 4:7). But his fight and his race weren't against his brothers. His goal was the courageous advance of the cause of Christ in a hostile environment. You can count on it, that when he crossed the finish line, he heard, "Well done, thou good and faithful servant."

One reason things often get so difficult among believers, so scrambled, so destructive, is that we forget that God has called us to something that is beyond ourselves, more important than ourselves—something of true ultimate and eternal significance.

Some of us need to get out of the amusement park and onto the highway.

DISPLACED PERSONS

The older we get—and we are all getting older—the more vitally important it becomes to feel safe and secure. We cherish familiar settings, places that are compatible to our relationships and lifestyle. In a culture that pushes us from here to there like tumbleweeds, familiarity protects our sanity and serenity. Change and displacement are always stressful and unsettling.

Walking the streets of our great city of Chicago, I see many displaced people. Some are homeless of their own doing, others through the winds of fate. They spend their days looking for a warm, quiet place to sleep and wondering where their next meal will come from.

And as the economy continues to unravel, creating fears about the future, others are finding that they have been displaced from their jobs. All the meaning and fulfillment they received from being productive in the work force has suddenly disappeared. They have no place to experience the worth and value of making a contribution through their careers.

Throughout history, wars have displaced sons and daughters, sometimes permanently. Natural disasters have displaced others. Cruel and oppressive regimes have spawned pilgrimages of many who found it necessary to leave the comforts of their native land and flee to unknown places from the tyranny of fear.

Whatever the cause, to most of us displacement is an unwelcome and unsettling prospect. It almost always means loss and sacrifice.

That's what strikes me about the wonder of what happened at Christmas. Think of the fact that God Himself, in the person of His own Son, Jesus Christ, was willing to dramatically displace Himself—to change places from the secure realms of the universe where His presence existed without limits. Think that God would volunteer to displace Himself from the grandeur of His glory and all the marvelous perks of paradise.

Christmas is about God sacrificing the privileges of reigning as Creator and King to incarcerate Himself into the body of a child and then take thirty-three years to walk this planet, rejected by His own, scoffed by His family, misunderstood by both political and religious leaders—and ultimately to be crucified on an instrument of ancient torture as a societal reject.

It seems almost incomprehensible, given what we know about the discomfort and despair of displacement, that God would displace Himself so readily and dramatically for us.

But isn't that the key—that He did it for us? If the cause were great enough, many of us might displace ourselves and endure the sacrifice and suffering it brings. That's why some volunteer to go to war. Why others leave family and friends to move to another location for a new ministry or career.

The stunning point of Christmas is that God considered my needs and the worth of my relationship to Him to be sufficient cause to go through the trauma of changing places. "For you know the grace of our Lord Jesus Christ," the apostle Paul wrote, "that though he was rich, yet for your sake he became poor, so that you by his poverty might become rich" (2 Corinthians 8:9).

Have you ever felt so loved, so cared for, as you do when you think of the profound meaning of Christmas? If we understand Christ as the most significantly displaced person of history—displaced for us—it is hard not to thrive in His embracing love for us.

Philippians 2 reminds us that Jesus Christ did not consider the glories of His divinity as something to cling to. Rather, He "made himself nothing, taking the form of a servant, being born in the likeness of men. And being found in human form, he humbled himself by becoming obedient to the point of death, even death on a cross" (Philippians 2:7–8).

Christ displaced Himself to guarantee for us a permanent place where eternally we can be secure, safe, and satisfied. A place where there is no fear of displacement or of unexpected change that would threaten our fulfilling experience in Him. God changed places that He might place us permanently in "the kingdom of his beloved Son" (Colossians 1:13).

This is the message and the meaning of Christmas. When you stop and think about it, its point is wonderfully profound. At the very center of the reason God became a displaced person, stand you and I.

In the words of the hymn writer, "Amazing love! How can it be, That Thou, my God, shouldst die for me?"

GETTING THROUGH

Years ago, telecommunication was a warm and friendly experience. Each telephone call meant ringing up a local operator, who then would personally place the call. For the curious, there was the party line—one telephone link that several families would share. In those days, the invention of Alexander Graham Bell was a people affair through and through.

As our technology grew more sophisticated, however, the experience changed. We no longer needed an operator to place our calls. And party lines gradually disappeared.

But each call, whether dial or touch-tone, still placed us in direct contact with people. Our primary frustration was the busy signal, which at least let us know that someone was alive and well at the other end.

The system was revolutionized years later when a federal judge's ruling split up the Ma Bell monopoly. Since then, our monthly bills have risen, and our confusion has multiplied. New companies now offer an array of competing programs that measure their advantages in fractions of pennies per minute.

Then came more "advances" in telephone technology. We now enjoy the privileges of talking to computers, being interrupted in the midst of significant conversations by call waiting, and leaving messages in the ever-present voice mailbox machines.

To those of us who are people persons, these computerized telephone responses often provide a distressing sequence of disappointment.

Recently, on my way to a well-known Christian organization, I discovered to my chagrin that I was lost. Rather than trying to bungle my way into deeper lostness, I decided to call for directions.

All I needed was a quick conversation with a real person, someone who could tell me where I was and how to get where I was going. Instead, I entered a maze of computer messages passing me from one place to another until I finally fell into a telecommunications trash bin.

Don't get me wrong. I appreciate the advantages of technological gain. It's just that with all of our sophistication, it's tough to get through. There's something distant and cold about modern telecommunications that compounds our societal sense of alienation and frustration.

As I was griping to myself about this one day, a thought came to mind: *Aren't you glad that heaven is still a user-friendly place?* Our Father in heaven is always there, always listening, and—through the Spirit and the Word—always willing to communicate with us. It's good to know that our prayers will never get dumped into a voice mailbox. And there are no call-waiting interruptions.

By redemption, we're all subscribers to the same efficient system. We are granted free, around-the-clock access lines regardless of race, color, or class.

What a refreshing and encouraging contrast to telecommunications on our planet!

But further reflection caused me to ponder how God views our use of His system.

How often, I wonder, does He hear a busy signal from us? He is the ever-present God who created us to enjoy communion and fellowship with Him. But given the busyness of our lives—a busyness compounded by the sophisticated technology that entertains us, computes for us, and communicates with us—we frequently don't have time to spend with Him.

And all too often, our brief times with the Lord are interrupted, as if we had installed a call-waiting mechanism in the communication lines.

Sometimes all He hears from us are rote, computer-like messages repeated time and time again with a ritualistic chill and a hollow, distant sound.

Could it be that when He seeks to speak to us in His still small voice, He gets only our voice mailbox?

"I'm sorry, but I'm away from my desk right now. If you would like to leave a message, please press 1. Or if you would like to speak to someone else, simply dial the extension number for that heart now . . . "

Communication is a two-way street. And while we revel in the reality that we can always get through to heaven, our concern should be whether our Lord can always get through to us.

No wonder God so often calls us away from the crush of our modern technological busyness to be still and know that He is God, to meditate on His Word and His works, and to pray without ceasing.

I'm thankful that He is fully accessible. I just wonder how well He's doing on getting through to me.

BETTER THAN WE DESERVE

Testimony meetings can be discouraging events for many of us who are just common folk, going through good times as well as bad, seldom seeing God's hand moving in dramatic ways. Compared to the spectacular accounts of the Lord's intervening power that we sometimes hear or read, our own lives seem rather drab and ordinary.

What makes those testimonies so discouraging is that they raise serious questions in our minds. Does God care for us as much as He cares for those who have such stellar stories? Is there something wrong with us, something that disqualifies us as miracle material?

Sometimes our discouragement deepens as we read the stories of great heroes of the faith. We find God leading Moses and the children of Israel through the Red Sea, sending them manna, giving them front row seats to watch the collapsing walls of Jericho. We see Him sending a great revival to Nineveh. We hear of the dramatic resurrection of Lazarus and the otherworld experiences of the apostle Paul in the third heaven.

Our experiences seem dull by comparison, and we end up wondering why we don't see similar evidence of God's dramatic work in our lives. It's not necessarily that we lack prayer or personal purity or faith. We pray earnestly for God to work, we seek to keep our lives pure before Him, and we truly believe He could do in us and through us whatever He desires. Yet we rarely see Him operate in extraordinary ways.

Before the cumulative effect of all this puts our hearts in the ditch, we need to remind ourselves of an important mathematical fact. When we add up God's dramatic interventions recorded in the Old Testament and divide them into the number of years in

Old Testament history, the net result shows that God rarely intervened in dramatic ways. Only in a few, unique moments did His eternal purposes demand a supernatural interruption in the ordinary flow of events.

In addition, we need to remind ourselves of God's regular, quiet, yet supernatural work in our lives. He, without our notice, sovereignly blocks that which would be too heavy to bear (1 Corinthians 10:13). He gives us the grace to endure difficulty, to remain positive in negative times, to show forgiveness and joy instead of bitterness. I think of friends like David Ring, who, despite cerebral palsy, is a dedicated and fruitful evangelist. Or Joni Eareckson Tada, who, from the wheelchair she is confined to because of her paralysis, radiates the love of Christ.

Our Lord not only works through relief or release but sometimes His greater grace is given to make us strong in weakness (2 Corinthians 12:9–10).

Even if there were nothing else, we must never forget that all of us who know Him are walking displays of the most spectacular, supernatural event in history—the transforming power of the cross of Christ.

It's the touch of redemption on our lives that is the most spectacular miracle of all. Hell has been canceled and heaven guaranteed. Once under the judgment of God, now we have His Holy Spirit living in us, guiding, reorienting, and enabling us daily. Old things have passed away, and all things have become new (2 Corinthians 5:17).

Every believer, no matter how "ordinary," carries the dramatic reality of eternal life and all its abundant privileges (John 10:10).

If God never does anything more than redeem us, He has already done far more than we deserve. That one act gives us enough to be grateful for every day of our lives. We have far more than even the children of Israel, whose Red Sea experience cannot compare to our redemption through Christ's blood.

Recently a friend asked me how I was doing. "Better than I deserve," was my reply. To which he said, "Oh, no. You deserve a lot."

But in reality the only thing I deserve is hell. Considering who I am in light of a holy and just God, heaven is an absolute impossibility—except for the gracious gift of Christ's redemption.

I'm reminded of the old Puritan who had been imprisoned for his faith. When his daily ration of stale bread and water arrived, he gladly exclaimed, "All of this and heaven, too!"

I received a note from a Moody alumnus, who, at 83 years of age, had obviously learned to recognize the hand of God on his life. After cataloging his blessings and burdens since leaving Moody, he concluded, "I'm 83 years old—walk with two canes. Been everywhere but heaven. Ready to go anytime. Have only one eye—see you there!"

Been everywhere but heaven! See you there!

Who could ask for more?

Before this month of March is past, we will have celebrated the resurrection of Christ, our guarantee of life and victory over death and hell.

If we are not careful, however, in the midst of our jubilation we will overlook the terrible pain in the process of Christ's victory.

No one has ever experienced the dimensions of His anguish—of rejection, misunderstanding, loneliness, and physical torture. All of this was compounded by the agony of the accumulated weight of all mankind's sin loaded on His heart.

In our world that is so addicted to comfort and ease and so intimidated by testing and trouble, we must remember that at the core of Christianity stands an instrument of torture. The agony of the cross, the inevitable result of the conflict between heaven and hell, was so real that Christ begged to bypass it and so significant that the Father could do nothing less than lead His Son through it.

The cross gives meaning to trouble that is both relevant and profound.

Job said, "Man is born to trouble as the sparks fly upward" (Job 5:7).

How true!

The trouble with life is that it's so daily!

For many, Murphy's Law often seems eclipsed by O'Toole's Law, which states that Murphy was an optimist.

Whether it is the relatively insignificant flat tire in a downpour or the despair that comes from broken health, lost wealth, or alienation in significant relationships, trouble and its pain are life's indiscriminate reality.

None of us is exempt.

Given our bent to expect that life owes us eighty years of pain-less bliss, it is not surprising that we often fall prey to the destructive responses of anger, bitterness, blame, vengeful plans, withdrawal, alienation, and the cold determination not to forgive.

But with these counterproductive responses, we make more trouble of the trouble that troubles us.

The suffering of Christ shows us a better and more authentic way, a way that leads to glory and gain through the pain.

The Easter season should give us the confidence that indeed our God is able to engineer every crisis, no matter how unfair, to cause all things to work together for good. The cross without the resurrection would be so incomplete, so unlike God, who ulti-mately brings glory from pain.

This Easter, as we again watch Christ's movements through His agonizing ordeal, we see a pattern of response that we should follow.

- Complete honesty before God as we admit that our pain seems more than we can bear and that we wish to be relieved of it (Matthew 26:37–39).
- A yieldedness that admits God's way, regardless of the pain, is best and that expresses our willingness to endure it for Him (Matthew 26:42).
- A loving commitment to the interests of others, even if it means suffering and sacrifice (Philippians 2:5–8).
- A decision to persevere, with a confidence in the ultimate application of God's justice and care (1 Peter 2:21–24).
- A wholehearted commitment to what God is producing in our lives that eclipses our commitment to comfort or personal pleasure (James 1:2–5).
- An unshakable resolve to obey our Lord in the midst of pain, regardless of the cost (1 Peter 1:21–22).

- An unwavering belief that God's grace is sufficient for any and every moment in our lives (2 Corinthians 12:9).

Actually, if we understood the tremendous damage that sin has wrought to this planet and its people, we would not be surprised by pain. We would be surprised that we ever experience seasons of comfort and peace and joy.

When pain does come our way, we have the magnificent opportunity to show a watching world what Christ showed the onlookers at the cross—the miracle of a life that demonstrates through faith, patience, confidence, and courage that God is sufficient to help in bad times as well as good.

I find great pleasure in the truth that God is moving all of life and history to that glorious moment when "He will wipe every tear from [our] eyes." In that day, "death shall be no more, neither shall there be mourning nor crying nor pain anymore, for the former things have passed away" (Revelation 21:4). We will live eternally beyond the intrusion of all that hurts us in this life.

But until then, may He find us faithful to the pattern of the cross.

OLDER OR BETTER?

Recently, I heard myself saying to a friend, "I can't believe this year has gone by so fast. It seems that the older I get, the faster time goes." As a child, I had always been curious when my parents said that; now I was saying the same thing.

There are many ways to know we're getting older. "Can you believe how young these professional ballplayers look?" we say. "They look like they're in high school."

It's a sure sign of aging when we no longer ask, "How are you?" but say, "Hey, you look terrific"—as if we're surprised.

I have a friend who says, "You know you're getting older when your back goes out more than you do . . . when you bend down to pick something up, and you stay down there to see if there's anything else you should get on this trip . . . and when all the names in your little black book end with M.D.

"Time marches on, and then one day you look in the mirror and you realize it's been marching across your face."

Aging is an inevitable fact of existence. Unfortunately, our society has taught us to fear advancing age and to disguise its reality at every opportunity.

The second most lucrative field of medicine in America is plastic surgery. Face-lifts, tummy tucks, and an array of other ways to reverse the signs of the aging process are in great demand. Dreaded mileposts along the way that create emotional havoc—aided by enthusiastic friends—are 40, 50, and 65. So we learn to view age as an enemy, not as a friend.

In this area, Christian thinking stands in direct contrast to the perspectives of society. In Christ we have the capacity to get significantly better, even while we grow older.

God's Word emphasizes that this spiritual maturing takes time—a lifetime. Just as there are physical signs to show that we are getting older, so there are biblical signposts to show us whether we are getting better.

We know we're getting better in Christ when our minds are being transformed from the values of the world. Romans 12:2 calls this aging process the "renewing of your mind." The maturing Christian mind views people, things, money, and ministry from God's perspective—instinctively growing better at forgiving, loving, caring, sharing, and witnessing to our faith in Jesus Christ.

Maturing believers groom their capacity to discern the differences between good and evil (Hebrews 5:12–14). We no longer need someone to tell us what is right and wrong because we have exercised our own understanding of scriptural principles. Periodically, I meet believers who mistakenly assume that age in Christ enables them to live with greater "freedom" in questionable behavior. But true maturity shuns evil and lives for what is good.

According to Ephesians 4:11–15, growing older in Christ means becoming more like Him. Why is it that with age we tend instead to become more crotchety, intolerant, unloving, and resistant to change? In Christ, we should be growing rich in character, demonstrating the fruit of the Spirit: love, joy, peace, patience, kindness, goodness, faithfulness, gentleness, and self-control (Galatians 5:22–23).

If spiritual aging involves the process of becoming more like Christ, then we should also have the attitude of Christ (Philippians 2:5). We should increasingly be willing to give up our rights and privileges to focus on the needs of others.

If we are actively engaged in the authentic process of biblical Christianity, we can become wonderfully and measurably better as the years go on.

In Christ, getting older also means getting nearer. Nearer to the culmination of our redemption in Jesus Christ. Nearer to the day when the weight of our fallenness will finally be lifted. When old things will finally pass away and all things become new.

All of life for the Christian is the process of preparation for what the apostle Paul calls "far better" (Philippians 1:23). The most significant thing about Paul's description of our eternal privilege is that he does not qualify the far-betterness. It is far better. Far better than anything we could know or experience in this fleeting existence. It is the grand and glorious privilege of not only knowing Christ but of seeing Him and being with Him—the one we love though we have not seen Him.

No wonder the hymn writer wrote, "When I tread the verge of Jordan, bid my anxious fears subside!" In Christ, getting older is getting better and nearer.

BULLISH ON HEAVEN

You've probably noticed we are living in boom times that are unprecedented in recent history. I had heard about it and read about it, but recently came face-to-face with it in full force.

While spending a weekend in Florida this past winter, I was playing golf with a friend and noticed the homes that were being built around the course and between the fairways. Actually, to call them *homes* would be a gross injustice. They were more like hotels in size and posh appointments. The architecture was dazzling and the landscaping lush. There were literally dozens of them.

I asked my friend where all the money comes from to build these multimillion-dollar monuments to luxury. He replied that there has been so much money made on the stock market, that people are cashing in and fulfilling their dreams.

If earth is your only destination, then that's probably a good idea. No one knows what the market is going to do. The variables make it anybody's guess. What will the Fed do to interest rates? What will ultimately happen to the markets in Asia? If everything is overvalued, will there be a catastrophic meltdown? Or will the Dow climb to 15,000 by January? Everyone has an opinion, and no one knows for sure.

If you are looking for a long-term investment strategy that is fail-safe . . . I have one for you. It's a strategy that was advanced in ancient times by a wandering peasant, and I know of no one who has followed His advice who has ever been disappointed. In fact, it was offered first in boom times that were so prosperous, people were planning to tear down their barns to build bigger ones to hold all their increase. It was a festive time in the land, and the word was out that this was the season to eat, drink, and be merry.

Still, this transient had a read on the recent upturn of the economy that had escaped everyone else's notice.

He observed that those who assume that true prosperity is measured in the currency of this present world are, as He put it, fools. Not fools because they had much, but fools because they had nothing of life's most important commodity. As He explained, life could disappear in a flash, transferring us immediately into eternity—where everything is confiscated at the border. Only those who carry the passport of a redemptive experience with God enter the joy of His presence. As He said, "What shall it profit a man, if he shall gain the whole world, and lose his own soul?"

He gave some very strategic insider advice to His followers, all of whom carried the passport. While you *can't* take it with you, He told them, you *can* send it on ahead. Earthly wealth invested in rescuing lives from hell and in advancing the eternal kingdom of God will pass through the currency exchange of heaven and will accrue to your eternal account.

This investment remains solid and sure. Heaven is real, and all that we invest in this everlasting portfolio will never collapse. Its returns are measured in the unparalleled gain of people's eternal destinies and the glory of His name through a spiritually powerful and effective church.

A friend and I were talking recently about the amazing run of the stock market and the vast amounts of new earth-side wealth that has been created. He observed that this could be a great season for the work of Christ. His assumption was that followers of Jesus who have benefited from today's economic prosperity would pass significant amounts of the surplus through to the cause of eternity.

In his words, "God may be able to accomplish great things in our day with the underwriting of these unprecedented resources." Ministries should flourish with capital to invest in programs and personnel. Missionaries long under-supported should finally be free to serve without distraction.

But here is the rub. Will we see this as a moment to advance the strategic cause of Christ? Or will we consume the gain on our own transient plans and pleasures, leaving the kingdom as the only entity that fails to benefit from this abounding affluence?

I'm bullish on heaven . . .

PART SIX

TAKE THE SWORD
OF THE SPIRIT

WITHOUT A CLUE?

Michael Drosnin's book, *The Bible Code,* has taken our insatiable curiosity for the mysterious by storm. Who would have dreamed it: secret codes locked in the letters and words of the Old Testament that, when decoded, reveal details of the future with remarkable precision?

I've always believed the Bible is a supernatural book. Yet I have to admit that even for this believer it's a stretch to imagine that God wanted to give our world a hidden code as added evidence of the authenticity of Scripture. That seems a futile endeavor since the Bible already carries the signature of the supernatural. Witness the remarkable accuracy of fulfilled prophecy, the unprecedented endurance of the text, and the relevance of its ancient wisdom even in our sophisticated, high-tech times. And if it is futuristic predictions that you are looking for, the Bible is full of dramatic scenarios of the end times.

For the sake of argument, let's say that Drosnin is on to something. Would a hidden code that unlocked future events be the ultimate, convincing proof to an unbelieving world that the Bible is of supernatural, divine origin? Would it lead legions of unbelievers to bow to its authority?

I doubt it. God is rarely embraced because the evidence weighs in His favor. God is denied because we do not want Him interfering in our lives. Why do otherwise well-educated people deny that there is a creator when all the evidence points to an intelligent design? Why do we cling tenaciously to theories that depend on the unlikely prospect of random chance producing highly sophisticated systems more intricate than anything our technology has been able to produce?

If we accept that the Bible is true and that the God of the Bible is really here, then we must also accept what He says about us: that we are sinners hopelessly and helplessly guilty before Him. That we are accountable for how we live our lives. That we are not capable in and of ourselves to deal with the ultimate dilemmas of life. That we need a Savior, and that we humbly must repent and gratefully restructure our lives to conform to His ways instead of our own.

Our hearts are not softened and our spirits are not humbled before God by dazzling predictions hidden under layers of codified intrigue. We come to realize that God is, and that we desperately need Him, through the work of the Holy Spirit and the clear statements of Scripture that need no clues to reveal their truth.

Christ had some clear words for those in His day who dodged their own responsibility before God by demanding more and more signs—as though what He had already done were not enough. He said, "An evil and adulterous generation seeks for a sign" (Matthew12:39). In another context He declared, "If they do not hear Moses and the Prophets, neither will they be convinced if someone should rise from the dead" (Luke 16:31).

Verifying that claim, His own resurrection failed to turn the world toward God, even though the divine feat was undeniably authenticated during forty days of post-resurrection appearances. In fact, after His ascension, only 120 devoted followers were left waiting for His promise of the Spirit.

It was not until Pentecost that the masses turned to God as the Spirit-empowered proclamation of the gospel penetrated otherwise recalcitrant hearts. The early church's people made an impact on their world of unbelief by unashamed communication of God's Word and an allegiance to it that led to righteous living.

The rewarding outcomes of applied Christianity stood in sharp contrast to the emptiness and despair produced by pagan permissiveness. Christians preached volumes by their willingness to die agonizing deaths for what they had found to be true and their unshakable belief in a better world to come.

There is a lesson here for us. Our hope to draw hearts to Christ rests not in veiled codes. It lies in the time-honored strategy of our personal commitment to what is clearly understandable and the authentication of that belief through lives that reflect peace, purposefulness, and righteousness.

HOW SWEET IT IS

When our children were young, Martie and I had the good fortune of having both sets of our parents live in South Florida. This enabled us to vacation there with little expense. If we could get there, nearly everything else was taken care of.

But that was the challenge—getting there. The strain of the 1,200-mile trip with children in the backseat—the crying, the fussing, the bickering, the "Dad, she's breathing" and "Mom, he crossed the line"—nearly drove us to distraction.

I often wonder if God doesn't feel a similar frustration. Something happens on our journey to paradise that erodes the love and unity of His children. The things that divide us are usually not worth fighting about, and certainly not worth injuring the reputation of Christ.

There's a refreshing wind blowing across the church today—the wind of unity. Brothers and sisters are discussing ways to work together in the body of Christ. It must delight our Lord, for one of His last commands was, "As I have loved you, you also are to love one another. By this all people will know that you are my disciples, if you have love for one another" (John 13:34–35).

Two principles are vitally important. First, unity is important, but it's not the most important thing. Second, unity is more important than almost anything else.

In His High Priestly prayer (John 17), Christ prayed that all believers would be one. That prayer, however, comes in the context of being set apart by the truth of God's Word (v. 17). Truth, the core orthodox doctrine embraced by the true church through the ages, can never be sacrificed on the altar of unity. In fact, truth is the basis for our unity: truth about the deity of Christ; that salvation comes by grace through faith alone, through Christ alone; that the Scriptures are the sole authority for faith and practice and inerrantly reliable. These are the unifying points to which we all come. At the center of these truths is the person of Jesus Christ. He and His cause have a marvelous way of lifting us above our lesser differences.

In addition, righteousness cannot be sacrificed on the altar of unity. We can never erode the distinction between good and evil. A unified church will love those who sin and seek to draw them to repentance and remediation, but ultimately—to protect the purity of the whole—it must separate itself from those who persist in sin. Orthodox doctrine and authentic righteousness do divide, but they strengthen the unity Christ calls us to.

Having said that, we must work to cross over differences that create costly, unnecessary divisions. This doesn't mean sameness. There are differences of gender, color, gifts, culture, temperaments, class, roles, perspectives, denomination, and doctrinal definitions. Christ did not call us to forget our differences, but to rise above them and find our oneness in His presence with us.

If we want God to work afresh in our time, we must cultivate a biblical tolerance. The tolerance that focuses on casting the beam out of our eyes rather than focusing on the weaknesses of others. The tolerance that bears the burdens of one another, is kind to one another, prays for one another, supports one another. This tolerance is built on servanthood rather than self-centeredness and self-enhancement. It needs to begin in each of our hearts, our homes, and our churches so that a watching world will know there is something dramatically different about following Christ.

Thankfully, Martie and I are past the stage of kids scrapping and bawling in the backseat. Our children are grown, married, and busy about their own lives. When we all get together now, there is a sense of harmony, joy, mutual appreciation, and affirmation.

Wouldn't you think Christians were grown up enough to know the difference between what is petty and what is strategic? Maybe that's just it. Though we've spent a lot of time in the kingdom and learned the theology and mastered the codes of behavior, perhaps we have never really grown up.

Christ must long for the day when He will hear His church say with joy, "Behold, how good and pleasant it is when brothers dwell in unity!" (Psalm 133:1).

TIME AND TEMPERATURE

On most mornings, my walk to the office takes me down the same streets, around the same corners, and across the same park. I pass Boston Chicken, turn left at The Gap, and then reach the dry cleaners. Across the street is a time-and-temperature clock, which in winter reminds me of why my face feels the way it does. It also quickens my pace to make up for lost time lingering with that earlier cup of coffee.

Time-and-temperature clocks are a dime a dozen. I had walked by this one for two and a half years, but it wasn't until last week that I noticed something unique about it.

It reminded me of the anonymous letter that I received soon after moving to Chicago and assuming my position at the Moody Bible Institute. In essence, the letter warned that if Moody did not contribute $100,000 to *The New York Times* fund for AIDS within seven days, then someone would gladly and without hesitation take my life.

Though it seemed like no more than a prank letter, MBI officials decided to show it to the special division of the Chicago police department that handles such matters. The police advised us to take the letter seriously.

That was certainly quite an unsettling thought!

Though I was not to tell my family about the threat, several security measures were implemented. During the next seven days, I didn't think much about the danger.

Until the seventh day. As I left the office to get in my car and drive to our home, which was then in the suburbs, I wondered if pulling the car door handle would trigger an explosion. Thankfully, it didn't.

I drove home remembering that my youngest son, Matthew, had been begging me to go bowling with him. Now I know that a lot of people like to bowl, but it has never been my favorite sport.

In addition, it was almost time for school to start. My wife, Martie, had suggested that I should go shopping with Matthew to help him pick out school clothes. Next to bowling, shopping for clothes is my least favorite pastime.

Fascinating how the thought that this could be my last night at home revolutionized my desires and plans. I walked in and asked Matt if he wanted to go bowling. I even shelled out a stack of quarters for Matt to play the video games. Then we headed to T. J. Maxx, where I made several trips between the clothes racks and the dressing room to help Matt complete his fall wardrobe.

As I fell asleep that night, I thought of what a dramatic difference it would make if I lived every day as if it were my last.

Which brings me back to my walk to the office. The strange thing about that time-and-temperature clock is that it's attached to a funeral home. I found myself thinking how appropriate it is for a time-and-temperature clock to be linked to a mortuary.

What time is it anyway? Our death is a good measure. And perhaps we ought to check our temperature regularly to see if the chill of death is looming nearer.

We have an uncanny way of living as if our tomorrows belong to us. We readily admit that death is inevitable, but rarely believe it could be imminent.

Reality says, however, that none of us has a guarantee on a time extension beyond this moment. At the end of this day, I could wake up and find myself finally home.

If I truly believed that this might be my last day, I would live it differently. I would talk to more people about Christ. I would spend more time in prayer with the One I was about to meet face to face. I would care more for Martie. Pour my life more into our kids. Be more patient and understanding with people around me and more supportive and sensitive to my colleagues.

Most of us believe we are living in the last days. Even better to believe that we may be living in our last *day*—and to live in the light of that reality.

I don't think the psalmist had a time-and-temperature clock in mind, but he did call us to this concept when he prayed, "So teach us to number our days, that we may present to You a heart of wisdom" (Psalm 90:12 NASB).

A COLLECTOR'S HEAVEN

Mankind seems to have a primal instinct to collect. There are collections of coins, canes, old cars, old toys, buttons, license plates, campaign paraphernalia, stamps, old books, old Bibles, cups and saucers, knives, spoons, dishes . . . the list is endless.

As a boy, I collected baseball cards. My sisters collected dolls. I find myself still drawn by the intrigue of collecting, though the objects are different.

Throughout the last century, the Staffordshire potteries in England struck small statues of influential people of the day. These common pieces of pottery were sold on the street corners for a small price and ended up in many English homes. Some of the statues represented Christian leaders like John and Charles Wesley and the great preacher, Charles Haddon Spurgeon. D. L. Moody and his musician, Ira Sankey, had such an impact in England that they, too, were included in the series.

Given my admiration for these men, my collecting urge was stirred. So we began looking for these figures on trips and in antique stores. My interest grew when I learned that the series also included great heroes of Scripture, like Moses with the Ten Commandments, Daniel in the lion's den, Elijah and the ravens, Christ with the children.

This will help you understand why a recent article in the *Chicago Tribune* caught my attention. It detailed the coming auction of the Ruth Flower estate. In the large, full-color picture that showed several of her collections, I noted some Staffordshire figures. My collecting instinct drew me to the auction house.

It didn't take long to discover that Ruth Flower had not collected any Staffordshire figures of my heroes. My wife and I spent the rest of the time browsing among the massive collections of antique furniture, silver, china, rugs, dolls, and dozens of other collections of things that, quite frankly, most of us would have never dreamed of collecting.

As I left the auction house, it struck me that collecting is so "earthside." One thing was clear that afternoon: Once we leave this earth, everything we own stays behind and becomes part of someone else's collection.

At that moment a wonderful truth set up residence in my heart. Speaking to His disciples who were consumed with earthside possessions, Christ said, "Lay up for yourselves treasures in heaven, where neither moth nor rust destroys and where thieves do not break in and steal. For where your treasure is, there your heart will be also" (Matthew 6:20–21). Those words reminded me of an eternal dimension for collectors: We can actually stockpile treasures for the world to come!

And Christ underscored that the treasures of the next world are more valuable than treasures here—so valuable that we should sell any earthly treasure that distracts us from eternal gain (Matthew 19:21).

Whether or not we're collectors on earth, it would be wise for all of us to examine what we're doing to collect treasures in heaven. The treasures of heaven are incorruptible. They never lose their worth. They can never be spoiled or stolen.

Scripture teaches us that we will receive the treasure of recognition in heaven for our earthly faithfulness, righteousness, sacrifice, and sufferings. Whether or not the "crowns" are literal objects to wear, they represent something tangible we receive to glorify and worship Christ. Revelation 4 portrays the elders, as an act of worship, casting their crowns at the feet of Christ.

Most of us would have a hard time giving up our earthside collections. But when we see Christ in heaven, we will look for every possible way to express our gratitude to Him. To live our life without laying up treasures in heaven would deprive us of one of the great privileges of eternity. How would we feel standing before Him with nothing to give?

Scripture also teaches that we should use our lives, and in particular our money, to rescue people from the eternal consequences of sin and lead them to heaven. In an interesting spin on that truth, Jesus Christ encourages us to use our money to make friends who will welcome us into heaven (Luke 16:9).

Think of stepping on shore and having one, two, several, many, come up and thank you for having invested in the work of God in their lives. Think of having an eternal collection of friends who will be a source of joy and satisfaction forever.

What value would it be to have collected much here—and little or nothing there? For all of us collectors, that's an important question.

NETLESSNESS

Ultimately, all of us are followers, even those who lead. Children follow parents. Teenagers follow peers. As adults, we follow fads and fashion, self-interests, instincts, principles, and plans. Every step of the way, we follow someone or something.

The issue of life is not will we follow, but whom will we follow, and where will that lead us?

One of the most intriguing sections of Scripture comes early in the Gospels. Christ, while walking by the Sea of Galilee, intercepts the lives of two fishermen brothers, Peter and Andrew. "Follow me," He says, "and I will make you fishers of men" (Matthew 4:19).

That, in and of itself, is not so amazing. We expect Christ to intercept our lives. We expect Him to call us to follow Him.

The startling reality is that "immediately they left their nets and followed him" (v. 20).

None of us would argue the importance of following Christ. He is the compelling Person of the universe, and He has the only cause worth living—or dying—for. Our resistance to following Him lies not in the rightness of His call but in what restricts us from it.

For Peter and Andrew, it was their nets. The text clearly says they had to leave their nets to follow Him. They couldn't have it both ways, to continue in their present pursuits and to follow Christ. Had they been unwilling to leave their nets, they would have been unable to follow Him.

For most of us, following Christ will not mean giving up our careers. It will, however, entail letting go of our nets, anything that hinders us from doing what He leads us to do or being what He leads us to be.

Those nets might include plans, dreams, relationships, money, things, bitterness, anger, prejudice, and pride. If all we have is our nets, they may seem worth clinging to. But when Christ walks along the beach of our lives and calls us to follow Him, the issue becomes a matter of values. What are these nets worth when compared to Christ?

If someone were to ask me if I like money, I'd have to ask, "Compared to what?" Compared to poverty? The answer is yes. But compared to Christ, there is no contest. I'll take Christ in a minute. Do I value my plans? Absolutely! Compared to a directionless life, I want my plans. But compared to Christ, there's no contest.

And what of the nets of our relationships? The crowd we run with? Our business associates? The one we are dating, who is dragging us down spiritually and compromising our followership? Do we value relationships? Of course. But the value of a non-negotiated relationship with Christ is of far greater value.

Do we value the comfort zones of being around "our own kind"? Of hanging out with people who know us, understand us, think like us, and talk like us? No doubt! But if that clubishness causes us to ignore or, worse yet, look down on other clusters of people, then we have ceased to be followers of Christ. Those who value Christ more than the comfort zone of their own kind drop the nets of prejudice and insensitivity and follow Him into the lives of people, groups, and neighborhoods where they have never walked before.

It's really a matter of values: Do we value the nets in our hands more than the compelling Person in our lives? Like children who climb into the car of an abductor for a lollipop leaving the love and security of their family, we may live as if our nets are of greater value than He is.

Netlessness is not only a matter of values; it's also a matter of outcomes. Think of Peter and Andrew at the end of their lives if they had not followed Christ. Perhaps they could have looked back on a great career in terms of the number of fish they caught or the amount of money they made. But they would have little to show for eternity.

Compare that outcome to a lifetime of following Christ. Think of joining forces with a handful of others who turned the world upside down for Him. These followers began a stream of redemptive proclamation that has flowed through the generations, a message that has turned millions toward heaven, reaching all of us who know the abundance of Christ through the indwelling Holy Spirit.

And think of the outcome of a life that refuses to follow Christ. As Jim Elliot said so well, "He is no fool who gives what he cannot keep to gain what he cannot lose."

Following Christ begins with dropping our nets of resistance. Followers will find their netless hands clasped firmly to His, their hearts singing, "Where He leads I will follow, I'll go with Him, with Him, all the way."

THE TOUGH PART

When Christ directed His disciples to "love one another" (John 13:34), it's safe to assume that the tough part was the *one another* phrase. Loving people who love us is not too hard. But those "one anothers" who misunderstand us or mistreat us pose a tremendous challenge.

Yet Jesus said that such love would mark us as His followers. "By this all people will know that you are my disciples, if you have love for one another" (John 13:35).

If we were all exactly alike and always met each other's expectations, this would be a cakewalk. Within the body of Christ, however, there is a multitude of diversity—in social, economic, and ethnic backgrounds as well as in temperament, perspectives, and cultural habits.

Did you ever note how dramatically diverse the disciples were? John was explosive, a "son of thunder" who once wanted to call down fire from heaven. Yet at other times, he was marvelously tender. Mix this temperament with Peter's outspokenness and erratic behavior, most obvious when he whipped out a sword and lopped off a soldier's ear.

Think of dropping a skeptic like Thomas into that crowd. Every time someone made a proposal, he would probably challenge it. If something went wrong, no doubt he would quickly remind you that he had "told you so."

Even more fascinating is the contrast between Matthew and Simon the Zealot. Matthew was a tax collector, an employee of the Roman Empire. The Zealots were one of the resistance movements that opposed Roman rule. Including Matthew and Simon in the same group was hardly a formula for achieving love and unity.

Yet the disciples worked together with a sense of peace and unified purpose. Their secret? They had found something beyond themselves.

Each one was first and foremost a follower of Christ. Christ was a compelling person who took them beyond their own interests. And His cause was a compelling cause that drew them to something bigger than themselves. In comparison to the privilege of following Christ and advancing the cause of eternity, their earthly differences paled into insignificance.

As long as the disciples focused on following Christ and advancing His cause, they displayed a dramatic sense of mutual love and concern. The same principle holds true for us. As followers of Christ, we are colleagues in the work of Christ.

While there will always be clusters of preference, based on cultural or ethnic differences or even minor theological issues, we need to remember that some things are more important than our diversity. In this way we display the joy and power of oneness to a world struggling for harmony.

Being part of an agenda beyond ourselves liberates us to complement each other rather than compete with each other. Matthew was able to take the message of Christ to his friends who had buddied up to Rome. And Simon the Zealot became Christ's representative to the resistance force.

While pastoring, I finally woke up to the fact that the pastor in the church across town, who used different methods and had a different perspective on ministry, was reaching people I'd never reach. When I realized that we were not competitors, I found it easy to love him—and far more difficult to criticize him.

Perhaps our problem lies in the fact that we have sold ourselves out to lesser agendas: agendas of our preferences, cultural habits, our ethnic pride, and ourselves. Christ takes us beyond all that lesser stuff.

In recent years, Martie and I have noticed that our family gatherings have taken on a new dimension. Our children, now grown, enjoy getting together and show genuine love and concern for each other. I must admit it was not always that way. There were times that I wondered if, given the right instrument of torture, they might not dismember each other.

Likewise, as we mature spiritually, we exhibit a growing capacity to care for and appreciate one another in the body of Christ, regardless of our differences.

We'll never all be like each other, and, quite frankly, we'll never always like each other. But if we are all mutually dedicated to this wonderful Person who is above and beyond us and to His cause that is far more important than anything within or between us, then we will learn the joy of loving, appreciating, and complementing one another for the advance of the kingdom and the glory of our Father in heaven.

THE GREAT RACE

The month of June brings many sure signs of summer: the sweet smell of cut grass, soft breezes, picnics, fireflies, thunderstorms, . . . and joggers.

This unique breed of humanity, forced to run circles in cramped indoor quarters during the winter, emerges with the first hint of spring and spends the summer dashing through neighborhoods and forests.

I have nothing against runners. Some of my best friends are addicted. I even tried the pursuit, waiting for that surge of ecstasy that my friends told me I would experience, only to find that the ecstasy came when I stopped running.

Though I have never seen a jogger smiling, apparently there is something fulfilling about running. Thousands train to run marathons. One friend of mine runs one hundred-mile races through mountainous terrain.

Recently a running friend handed me an article from *Runner's World* that had a picture of D. L. Moody. It traced the origins of the nation's oldest race to the school he founded in Northfield, Massachusetts. The Hares and Hounds Race, which began in 1886, covered fourteen miles. The article said the school's emphasis on running tied in with Mr. Moody's commitment to the work ethic.

While Mr. Moody's picture and name did seem strange in *Runner's World* magazine, I realized that if he were here today, he would have a lot to say about running. My guess is that he would want to talk more about the race that Christians run than the Hares and Hounds dash.

The Bible often speaks of living out the Christian life as if it were a race. Every true disciple of Christ is a runner. The issue is not whether we will run, but how we will run.

"Run that you may obtain [the prize]," the apostle Paul wrote (1 Corinthians 9:24). Runners run to win, and winning requires discipline. Therefore, we must train ourselves in the disciplines of prayer and the Word. Runners who refuse proper nourishment or ignore the instructions of their trainer are inherently weak.

The biblical race, like all races, involves guidelines and boundaries. Paul committed himself to running by the rules. He did not want to be disqualified for the prize (v. 27). As good runners, we know the rules and gladly submit to them.

Scripture also teaches that those who run the race must lay aside every hindering weight (Hebrews 12:1). Even in cold weather, good runners strip down to the minimum of clothing. And the clothing they wear is light. If somehow we could see the spiritual race, we would notice that many of us run under layers of restrictive clothing and with heavy bags on our shoulders. Do we think we can win under the load of sin and self-centeredness?

Running for Christ means stripping down to the bare minimum, racing with pure hearts and lives unladen with willful sin.

Hebrews 12:1 goes on to say that this race requires perseverance. The word *perseverance* literally means the capacity to "remain under." Races are stressful. Sometimes the elements bring stress; sometimes it's the wind pushing against us; sometimes it's the weakness in our body; sometimes it's the mud kicked in our face from the runner in front of us.

The Christian's resolve is to persevere regardless—to run this race undaunted by any adversity, unexpected intrusion, or careless attitude of others who run with us.

And we run this race not for the praise and glory of men, not for our own self-satisfaction, and not for blue ribbons and prizes to display in the trophy case of our soul. *We run for Him.* We run together for Christ—for Christ's glory and for the honor of His name. We run for the advancement of His kingdom, the rescuing of lost souls, the rearing of godly families, the encouragement of fellow runners.

We run together for Christ. The race is often crowded with weary runners, and the strong are called to come alongside: to hold, to help, and sometimes to carry their brothers and sisters to the finish.

There is no other race like this one. It is, in both substance and outcome, the greatest and most strategic race that is and ever will be run in the history of this planet.

We've all been enlisted, and the stands are crowded with spectators. They gaze intently to see if this race called Christianity is all it's cracked up to be, wondering if they should join as well.

So run we will. We run, that at the end we can say, "I have finished the race, I have kept the faith. Henceforth there is laid up for me the crown of righteousness" (2 Timothy 4:7–8).

GOING FORWARD IN A
BACKWARD WORLD

I prefer to sit near the front of an airplane. It's not that I want to reach my destination before the other passengers; it just makes disembarking a little quicker.

On one recent flight, I was delighted to note that my seat assignment was in the first row. When I boarded, however, to my chagrin the first row had its back toward the cockpit. I was facing the other passengers.

I accepted my predicament and strapped on the seat belt. But as the plane headed down the runway, I found it awkward and unsettling to be lifting off facing backward.

Doing anything backward is uncomfortable, unpredictable, and sometimes disastrous. Walking backward, driving backward, and even looking in the mirror to put on a tie can be challenging. But consider how much of life is backward:

- When you have money to buy a house large enough for your family, your children have moved out.
- When you are wise enough to rear children, yours are grown and you're too old to have more.
- When you have experienced enough of life to know you need an education, your formal training is done.

Maybe it's a result of the fall, but whatever the reason, it seems that much of life is backward—mostly in areas we can't help or change.

At least we can take comfort that everyone else lives in the same backward world. We all have to adjust and do our best to beat the odds.

More troublesome to me is that we as God's people often live backward spiritual lives. Here is an area that we can—and must—change.

Scripture says this world is under Satan's control (John 14:30), its ethical structure opposed to the principles and practices of God. From God's point of view, the standards of the world are backward.

When we are seduced into living by the adversary's principles instead of God's, we leave our lives and our churches in a backward, defeated state.

Why is it when we think of

- *success,* we think of cars, houses, social circles, vacations, and material treasures?
- *power,* we think of climbing, outsmarting, manipulating, outmaneuvering, and conquering?
- *prestige,* we think of position, trophies, titles, and even places in church bureaucracies?
- *pleasure,* we think of being free to do all we want to do?
- *trouble,* we resist at all costs, consider it an enemy and permit it to embitter us?

I am struck by the words of God spoken through Isaiah: "For my thoughts are not your thoughts, neither are your ways my ways" (55:8).

Backward living comes naturally. It is the product of our fallen nature. Without the teaching of God's Word and the discipline to screen our thoughts and actions through the grid of God's truth, we fall into it automatically.

Our challenge is to think and live biblically—to go forward in a backward world.

What is success? Servanthood (Matthew 20; Philippians 2). Whatever our place, influence, or position, we are to serve God and men with true motives and a loyal spirit. Success with God will be evident when we hear that divine compliment: "Well done, good and faithful servant."

What is power? Yieldedness (Acts 1:8; Ephesians 5:18–21). True power comes from yielding to the will of God. It is when we are in His place, fulfilling His purposes, that His power fills us, allowing us to accomplish great things for Him. It is only when I displace myself from His will that I need to resort to the power games that ultimately sap me of my strength.

What is prosperity? Investing in eternity (Luke 12:13–34). Jesus consistently calls us to invest in treasures that do not grow old. Paul told Timothy that true prosperity is being godly and content with what we have (1 Timothy 6:6–19). Prosperity is measured in our generosity, our kindness, our willingness to assist those in need. When we invest in eternity, we are free to enjoy the good things God has given us on earth (Philippians 4:12).

What is pleasure? Righteousness (Psalm 1; John 15). The fleeting enjoyment of doing whatever we wish cannot compare to the pleasure of doing what is right. Righteousness brings peace and joy to replace the guilt, fear, and anxiety unrighteousness brings.

What is trouble? The fire that forges character (James 1:1–8). God uses trials to shape us into the image of His Son.

Sound backward? Perhaps this is something of what it means to be a fool for Christ's sake. Actually, it is the fool who has said in his heart, "There is no God."

So who is the fool? Not the one who is willing to live his life backward for God.

CLOSED FOR INVENTORY

Just when we thought the world was again becoming safe for preaching, headlines burned with a sad and startling story of a fallen brother. Those too-often-told stories have had measurable fallout, both within and without the body of Christ.

For those on the outside, the cynicism and suspicion with which they already view the church has been given a boost.

And what of us?

I don't know of a time when friends of mine who are Christian leaders have seemed more sobered. Many believers are asking probing questions that beg for answers.

Why do so many fall?

How can one preach with passion and sincerity against sin, yet live in its bondage?

I went to a neighborhood store recently to pick up a few essentials, only to find a sign that said, "Closed for Inventory."

It's inventory time for us. It's time to take serious stock. The church needs to ask, *and answer,* the tough questions. We need to adjust our armor and formulate our strategy more effectively.

I find myself asking, *Is there something within our system that tends to produce neatly packaged products looking for a place to fall?*

Some time ago, I was chatting with a man who consults with some of the largest U.S. companies about their quality control. Because ministry is a form of human quality control, I thought I'd ask him for some insights.

He said, "In quality control, we are not concerned about the product." I was surprised.

But then he went on to say, "We are concerned about the process. If the process is right, the product is guaranteed."

How relevant to our Christianity.

We tend to be more oriented to the "product" of our faith than the process.

As American Christians, we tend to desire and demand products of righteousness, but give little attention to the process.

Scripture, however, points to the need to devote our time and energies to the process.

Paul seeks a lofty goal for individual Christians in Philippians 1: "That you may approve what is excellent, and so be pure and blameless for the day of Christ, filled with the fruit of the righteousness that comes through Jesus Christ, to the glory and praise of God" (vv. 10–11). Notice that Paul prays that their lives will be characterized by excellent choices, which will lead to personal purity, which in turn brings about productivity, which then brings praise and glory to God through their lives. What a product! It doesn't get much better than that.

Yet all of that grows out of the *process* that Paul describes in verse 9, "that your love may abound more and more, with knowledge and all discernment." It is the process of a personal commitment to love, knowledge, and discernment. And the grammar indicates that the product is wholly dependent on the process.

Of the three elements in the process, knowledge is our forte. We as evangelicals are a creedal community. Our commitment to sound doctrine is unwavering.

Paul, however, marries the values of love and discernment to truth. He says truth cannot be understood apart from its benefit to others and the wisdom to apply it.

In all our talk about theology (dispensational theology, covenant theology, practical theology, biblical theology, exegetical theology, and systematic theology), we need to raise the flag for a *values theology.*

This is a theology in which we cannot divorce belief from behavior. Such a doctrinal system demands more of us than just assent to certain creeds. Values theology demands that our beliefs embrace a commitment to the ethical and moral ramifications of what we claim to be true.

When Paul wrote to the Corinthians, "You are not your own, for you were bought with a price" (1 Corinthians 6:19–20), he was affirming the theology of redemption. But he did not make that affirmation in a vacuum. He presented it within the context of living a life of moral purity that honors God with our bodies.

Can we truly say we believe in redemption if we don't believe we should live in a way that honors the God who redeemed us? As James says in his second chapter, true belief makes a difference in our behavior.

In the same vein, can we claim to believe in the truth of God's mercy if we fail to present our bodies as a living sacrifice (Romans 12:1–2)?

Are we truly Trinitarians if we refuse to be mutually submissive one to another, maintaining the equality and worth of each individual, regardless of our assigned roles (Ephesians 5–6; Philippians 2:4–11)?

A theology that is oriented toward values takes us beyond creed to consecration. It measures us not by what we know, but by what we are known. It refuses to grant a divorce to belief and behavior.

Values theology! Don't leave home without it.

REFERENCES

PART ONE: Having Fastened On the Belt of Truth

Is God Cute, or What?—November/December 1997

Is It the Gift or the Giver?—May/June 1998

Support the Troops!—April 1991, revised for Strength for the Journey Web site, May 28, 2007

Dealing with the "D Word"—January/February 1996

From Virtues to Values and Back Again—April 1995

The Truth about Unity—September/October 1999

Surrendering to the Interruptions—February 1995

The Test of Relevance—October 1994

In Spirit and in Truth—April 1994

Getting It Straight—March 1994

Pleasure Seekers—September 1993

Just Like Heaven—July/August 1993

Feeling Worse about Ourselves—May 1993

Followers Are Leaders—October 1992

We the People—September 1992

Now That's Significant—June 1992

Family—September 1991

Fingerprints of God—March 1989

PART TWO: Having Put On the Breastplate of Righteousness

Bless the Boundaries—May/June 1997

Seeing Beyond the Style—July/August 1995

With Runner's Eyes—July/August 1994

Murphy's Law—November 1993

What Might Have Been—November 1992

PART FIVE: Take the Helmet of Salvation

PART SIX: Take the Sword of the Spirit

NOTE TO THE READER

The publisher invites you to share your response to the message of this book by writing Discovery House Publishers, Box 3566, Grand Rapids, MI 49501, USA. For information about other Discovery House books, music, or videos, contact us at the same address or call 1-800-653-8333. Find us on the Internet at http://www.dhp.org/ or send e-mail to books@dhp.org.